The Relationship Revolution

The Relationship Revolution

Mastering 1:1 Account-Based Management

Sloan Newman

The Relationship Revolution: Mastering 1:1 Account-Based Management

Cover design by Sara Watson

Interior design by S4Carlisle Publishing Services, Chennai, India

First published in 2026 by
Business Expert Press, LLC
222 East 46th Street, New York, NY 10017
www.businessexpertpress.com

ISBN-13: 978-1-60649-314-4 (paperback)
ISBN-13: 978-1-60649-315-1 (e-book)

Marketing Collection

First edition: 2026

10 9 8 7 6 5 4 3 2 1

EU SAFETY REPRESENTATIVE
Mare Nostrum Group B.V.
Doelen 72
4831 GR Breda
The Netherlands
gpsr@mare-nostrum.co.uk

Contents

List of Figures vii
Foreword ix
Acknowledgments xi
Introduction xiii
Chapter 1 The Soul of Strategic ABM 1
Chapter 2 The Strategic Pivot to 1:1 ABM 7
Chapter 3 Designing the Bespoke Experience 31
Chapter 4 Identifying and Selecting Your Strategic Accounts 57
Chapter 5 Deep Account Intelligence and Understanding 79
Chapter 6 Crafting the Bespoke Account Experience 97
Chapter 7 Implementing 1:1 ABM Operations 121
Chapter 8 Real-Life Success Stories and Lessons Learned 147
Chapter 9 Measuring Impact and Scaling for the Future 171
Chapter 10 What Does It All Mean? 191

Bibliography 195
About the Author 199
Index 201

List of Figures

Figure I.1 ABM timeline xv
Figure 1.1 Three R's of ABM 4
Figure 2.1 Types of ABM and with investment/ROI 14
Figure 2.2 Lead Gen funnel versus ABM funnel 22
Figure 3.1 Sales ABM questionnaire 47
Figure 4.1 Ideal strategic account profile for ABM framework 59
Figure 4.2 Ideal Strategic Account Profile Worksheet 72
Figure 4.3 Potential ABM account selection 78
Figure 6.1 Strategic ABM timeline 111
Figure 7.1 Quote from sales regarding ABM 130
Figure 7.2 Maslow's hierarchy of strategic ABM needs 133
Figure 7.3 Martech landscape 137
Figure 8.1 The rhetorical triangle 151
Figure 8.2 ABM and CLV 159
Figure 9.1 Formula for net profit margin 178

Foreword

Reading *The Relationship Revolution* made me think and reflect not only on my own journey in account-based marketing (ABM) but also how we market, and most importantly why we market. In a world overflowing with artificial intelligence (AI), automation, digital platforms, and performance dashboards, it's easy to forget that ABM was never about technology. It was, and still is, about people.

This book reminded me of that fact and why 10 years on, I'm still just as excited about ABM. What struck me most about Sloan's book is how deeply it captures the essence of ABM as both a mindset and a movement. It's not a program or a campaign; it's a philosophy that places relationships at the heart of growth. Strategic ABM demands that we slow down, listen harder, and act with intent. It asks us to look beyond metrics and see the humans behind every logo—to understand what they care about, what they struggle with, and what success looks like for them.

In today's marketing landscape, everyone claims to "do ABM." Every platform, every agency, every software demo is built around it. But as Sloan Newman so powerfully shows in these pages, ABM is not something you buy—it's something you become. It's not the tech stack or the targeting algorithm that defines success; it's the culture of collaboration, empathy, and strategic clarity that lives inside the teams who practice it.

That distinction is critical.

Because while digital tools and data help us scale, it's the people within our organizations—the marketers, sellers, and leaders—who determine whether ABM fulfills its true purpose. When we invest in people first and create a shared vision while holding ourselves accountable for building trust, we lay the foundation for genuine, long-term partnerships with our clients. And those partnerships, in turn, fuel sustainable growth.

This book doesn't just explain how to execute ABM; it restores faith in what marketing can be when it's done with care, curiosity, and conviction. It's both a practical guide and a quiet challenge to return to the human center of our craft.

For me, *The Relationship Revolution* is a timely reminder that growth doesn't come from chasing trends or platforms. It comes from purpose, people, and the courage to build relationships that last.

Rachael Bell
Vice President, Account-Based Marketing, NTT DATA

Acknowledgments

Writing this book has been one of the most challenging and rewarding journeys of my professional life. It would not have been possible without the unwavering support, guidance, and inspiration of many incredible people in my life.

First and foremost, I want to express my deepest gratitude to **my wife, Melissa Newman**, whose patience, love, encouragement, and brilliance have been the foundation of everything I've accomplished. To my family, especially **Katherine Newman**, **Megan Buettner**, **Todd Newman**, **Carey Porter** and all the Newmans, Porters, and Forsts, thank you for your understanding, love, support, and belief in me—even during the long nights and early mornings when I was buried in drafts, books, and research.

I dedicate this work to the memory of **my father, Lloyd N. Newman**, whose wisdom, insights, and understanding continue to guide me daily. His influence shaped not only the person I am but also the principles that underpin this book.

To my **mentors—Gayle Duffy**, **Niall Caldwell**, **Rachael Bell**, **Bev Burgess**, and **Jennifer Robinson**—thank you for challenging my thinking, pushing me to grow, and showing me how to combine strategy with empathy in both marketing and leadership. Your lessons have been invaluable.

To **Rachael Bell**, your insights have helped me understand that ABM is not just a marketing strategy but a transformative approach to growth, collaboration, and value creation.

A special acknowledgment goes to **Christopher Davis, VP, Revenue Marketing at LevelBlue**. I would not have taken on this journey without his guidance, encouragement, and willingness to take time for me.

To my **peers and colleagues**, especially **Megan Stewart**, **Evan Jordan**, **Hannah Holloway**, **Stacy Celano**, **Kyle McGrotty**, **Fernando Costantino**, **Hannah Noah**, and **Caroline Staiger**, thank you for sharing insights, debates, and experiences that refined the practical perspectives captured in these pages.

To my teachers and academic influences, at **London Metropolitan University**, **École Supérieure de Commerce et Management**, **College of Charleston**, and **Glenforest High School**, whose passion for knowledge and critical inquiry shaped my desire to learn—thank you for laying the intellectual concepts that made this possible. Special thank you to **Professor Donald Nordberg** for always being there to chat and challenge my ideas.

And finally, I would like to recognize **Declan Mulkeen** and his *Let's talk ABM* podcast, which stimulated the idea for this book. The conversations, insights, and shared experiences from our interview helped crystallize many of the ideas and frameworks explored here. Declan's series continues to elevate the global ABM community and continues to inspire practitioners and thought leaders alike, including me.

Each of you has contributed, directly or indirectly, to this book and to my journey in understanding the art and science of strategic ABM. I am deeply grateful.

With sincere appreciation,

Sloan Newman

Introduction

ABM is just good marketing—with the courage to go deep instead of wide. A truth I learned not from theory, but from practice.

When I began my career in marketing, ABM wasn't on my radar. I knew how to write compelling copy. I knew how to pitch creative ideas and manage campaigns across channels. I knew how to handle clients. But developing a marketing strategy for a single account? That sounded inefficient—until it became essential.

Somewhere along the way, I started actively listening to the client and sales. I noticed that not all accounts were created equal. Some weren't just opportunities—they were long-term bets. Strategic relationships. Quiet giants. The accounts we understood best, invested in most deeply, and supported. They didn't just convert—they grew. And when they grew, so did we.

That's when I found Strategic ABM. Or maybe more truthfully—*it found me.*

Roughly a year ago, I joined Declan Mulkeen on his *Let's talk ABM* podcast to discuss customer-focused ABM. What began as a casual conversation turned into something bigger: a realization that much of what makes Strategic or 1:1 ABM so powerful—its emotional intelligence, its relationship-building, its deep listening—still isn't being talked about enough. That conversation lit the spark in my brain for this book.

Why I Wrote This Book

This book is a reflection of decades of personalized marketing and Strategic 1:1 ABM in real-world settings: late-night proposal reviews, whiteboarding sessions in hotel lobbies, executive videos recorded in a single take, and campaigns built on nothing more than a breakthrough in insight and a lot of belief.

It's not a theory book. It's not a playbook, either—though there are plenty of plays inside. It's a storybook, a workbook, and a blueprint for marketers, sellers, and leaders who want to do work that matters with the accounts that matter most.

I wrote it because ABM changed how I think about marketing—and how I think about people. And I wanted to share what I've learned in a way that feels real, accessible, and—hopefully—inspiring. Also, I've been working in what is now called Strategic ABM since 2006, when I wrote my postgraduate dissertation, "Podcast Advertising: Women's Attitudes Toward the Evolution of Pod-Ads." That was only about three years after Momentum ITSMA and Bev Burgess officially named personalized marketing as ABM and a decade before Strategic ABM would receive its proper definition. See Figure I.1 for the timeline.

Although my research primarily focused on business-to-consumer (B2C) audiences, it also examined how brands were cultivating long-term relationships with their audiences, drawing inspiration from Kevin Roberts's concept introduced in *Lovemarks: The Future Beyond Brands.*[1] Roberts argued that traditional notions of marketing and branding were becoming obsolete and that successful brands of the future would need to inspire "loyalty beyond reason" by forming deep emotional connections with consumers. My research explored a then-nascent area in 2007—how companies were using advertising on emerging digital platforms to align themselves with content relevant to audiences capable of becoming long-term customers, driven more by emotional desire than rational reasoning.

Nearly 20 years later, my work continues to center on building enduring relationships through marketing strategies designed to strengthen engagement with targeted accounts and drive significant revenue growth. The results of my dissertation research found that audiences were far more likely to remember advertisers offering products relevant to the content of the videocast—referred to as vlogs in 2007—and that participants were nearly twice as likely to consider a brand advertising on a podcast than one that was not.

---

[1]Roberts (2024).

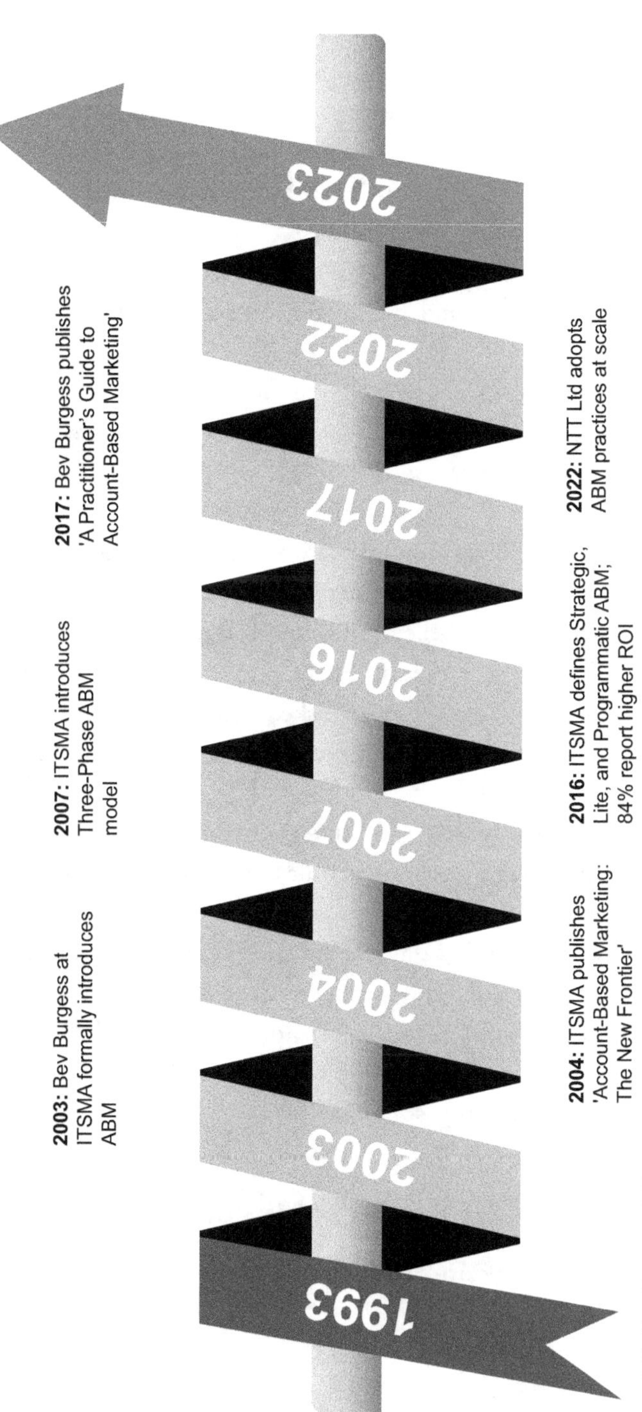

Figure I.1 ABM timeline

Who This Book Is For

- **Strategic marketers** who are tired of chasing marketing-qualified leads (MQLs) and want to build trust instead
- **Sales leaders** looking to partner more meaningfully with marketing
- **Chief Marketing Officers (CMOs)** and **Vice Presidents (VPs)** building ABM teams and looking for real examples, not just frameworks
- **New ABMers** who want to avoid the mistakes we've all made
- **Experienced practitioners** who want to elevate what they're doing and what they're measuring

And honestly, this book is for anyone who believes business isn't just about conversion—it's about connection.

If you're someone who believes that marketing is more than lead generation ... if you've seen the gap between sales and marketing firsthand and want to close it ... if you're tasked with growing top-tier accounts and building credibility with executive buyers ... you're in the right place.

Whether you're just launching a Strategic ABM program or looking to refine a mature strategy, this book is your blueprint in building a division that drives impact *and* earns trust.

We'll map out everything from account selection to stakeholder mapping, from customer relationship management (CRM) challenges to AI augmentation. But most of all, we'll focus on how to **build the kinds of relationships that last**, because in a noisy, complex, rapidly evolving marketplace—that's what truly scales.

What You'll Find Inside

Each chapter of this book explores a key component of Strategic or 1:1 ABM, including:

- Understanding what Strategic ABM really is (and isn't)
- Selecting the right accounts (and the right people)

- Building insight-driven narratives that create trust
- Designing bespoke experiences that actually land
- Operationalizing your ABM practice at scale
- Partnering with sales in ways that matter
- Measuring what really counts (Hint: It's more than revenue.)
- Embracing the future with AI, automation, and empathy
- And above all—**being clear**

Throughout the book, I've included personal reflections, client stories, real-life ABM wins (and misses), frameworks I actually use, and lessons I've learned from the best mentors, teams, and even competitors in the field.

One Last Thing Before We Start

ABM isn't about perfection. It's about **intention**.

This book is meant to make you think and not just provide you finite answers. It does have some answers but the thing with this level of ABM is that you will always need to be adapting to what your target account's needs and what messaging and content resonates the best with your audience. You should walk away from this book with clear ideas of what you want to accomplish with your Strategic account-based management program. In this book we will refer to ABM as account-based marketing, but I equate what Strategic ABMers to be more than just marketing. You will find that in Strategic ABM, you step into the role of CMO for a target account. And that means that you may find yourself doing so much more than just developing the marketing. If you are very good, you will find yourself presenting your content directly to the client leadership to get their feedback. You will be managing the marketing for your strategic target accounts.

In ABM, you don't need a perfect tech stack, a huge team, or a viral idea. You need the courage to care deeply about a few accounts; to learn everything you can about them; and to show up over and over with value, empathy, and clarity.

CHAPTER 1

The Soul of Strategic ABM

Always look at their shoes.

Lloyd N. Newman, Former VP of MS&L, NY,
and President of Newman Partnership, Ltd.

Let's Begin

That was the first real piece of business advice I ever received. I was 14, walking through New York City with my father, a seasoned public relations (PR) executive. We stopped near one of those classic shoeshine stands near Saks Fifth Avenue in New York City. I had asked him why there were such large chairs on the side of the street; he told me that it was where people had their shoes shined. He looked at them for a moment and then said,

> Whenever I meet someone, the first thing I do is look at the shoes they are wearing. Suits, smiles, and titles can all be part of the performance—but shoes are a personal thing. People who are comfortable making decisions don't dress to impress; they dress with intention. And more often than not, the person with the nicest shoes is the decision maker.

At the time, it sounded like one of those bad dad jokes or corny pieces of advice a father tends to give, like "don't trust a man with a weak handshake." But over time, I came to understand exactly what he meant. The details—the ones people think don't matter—often reveal the most about how they approach business, relationships, and trust. This story still shapes how I view marketing and client relationships. It's not about the flashy campaigns or big ideas pitched in a deck. It's about how you show up—consistently, thoughtfully, and attentively.

That, in essence, is ABM.

From Broad Campaigns to Bespoke Conversations

Strategic ABM returns us to something simple and powerful: **human connection**.

There's something sacred about giving your full attention to one person or one company. That's what Strategic 1:1 ABM demands. It asks us to slow down, to actively listen, and to move from messaging to meaning. And that requires a different mindset.

We live in a world awash in content, newsletters, e-mails, channels, and tools. But somewhere in the pursuit of scale and automation, many marketers and organizations have lost sight of what truly moves the needle: human connection. Strategic ABM or 1:1 ABM is a return to that guiding principle. It's the marketing equivalent of sitting down with someone, looking them in the eye, and saying, "I understand what matters to you, and I'm here to help you accomplish your goals."

"The 1:1 future will be characterized by customized production, individually addressable media, and 1:1 marketing, totally changing the rules of business competition and growth."[2] When Don Peppers and Martha Rogers, PhD, wrote these words in the first pages of *The One to One Future: Building Relationships One Customer at a Time* (1993, 5), they weren't just predicting the evolution of marketing—they were defining it. Their vision of personalized connection and customer intimacy foreshadowed a world where relevance would become the ultimate competitive advantage.

Today, that vision lives on through Strategic 1:1 ABM. What began as a consumer-centric idea of treating every customer as an individual has matured into a business-to-business (B2B) discipline that blends data, creativity, and human insight. In this new era, personalization is no longer a tactic—it's a strategy for building trust, accelerating growth, and shaping the relationships that define business success.

Strategic 1:1 ABM is not a trend. It's not a marketing technology (martech) use case. It's a philosophy executed by people who understand and recognize the complexities of relationships.

Some might argue that Marcel Bleustein-Blanchet was attempting to create human connection with brands through marketing in 1926 when

---

[2]Rogers (1993).

he founded Publicis, crafting personalized campaigns for individual clients. ABM simply gave the discipline a name—and more recently, a technology stack.

Organizations that are succeeding in the ABM space today are the ones that recognize it isn't just about targeting or verticalization—it's about teamwork. Not just about content—it's about creating relevant meaning, thought leadership, and value. And certainly not just about clicks, impressions, or engagement—it's about creating earned trust that leads to mutual growth. To paraphrase Peppers and Rodgers conclusion, 'the market is ripe for a revolution.'[3]

The Three R's That Matter Most

The foundation of this book rests on what Momentum ITSMA and Bev Burgess of The Inflexion Group have coined as the three R's of ABM (Figure 1.1):

Reputation. Relationships. Revenue.

But these are more than just metrics to track—they are the DNA strands of Strategic 1:1 ABM:

1. **Reputation** is how you show up in the market and how your clients talk about you when you're not in the room. How they view you and what they understand about the value that your organization, service, or product offers. The question to consider is: Are we changing how the account perceives us?
2. **Relationships** are built over time, with empathy, consistency, and insight. They are the most defensible advantage in B2B today. This tends to be the most difficult to quantify and the most important variable when it comes to winning. The question to ask is: Are we building and deepening connections?
3. **Revenue** is not the end goal but the by-product of getting the first two right. Too many of us are hamstrung by the argument that if the revenue comes through, then the campaign was a success. I will

[3]Ibid.

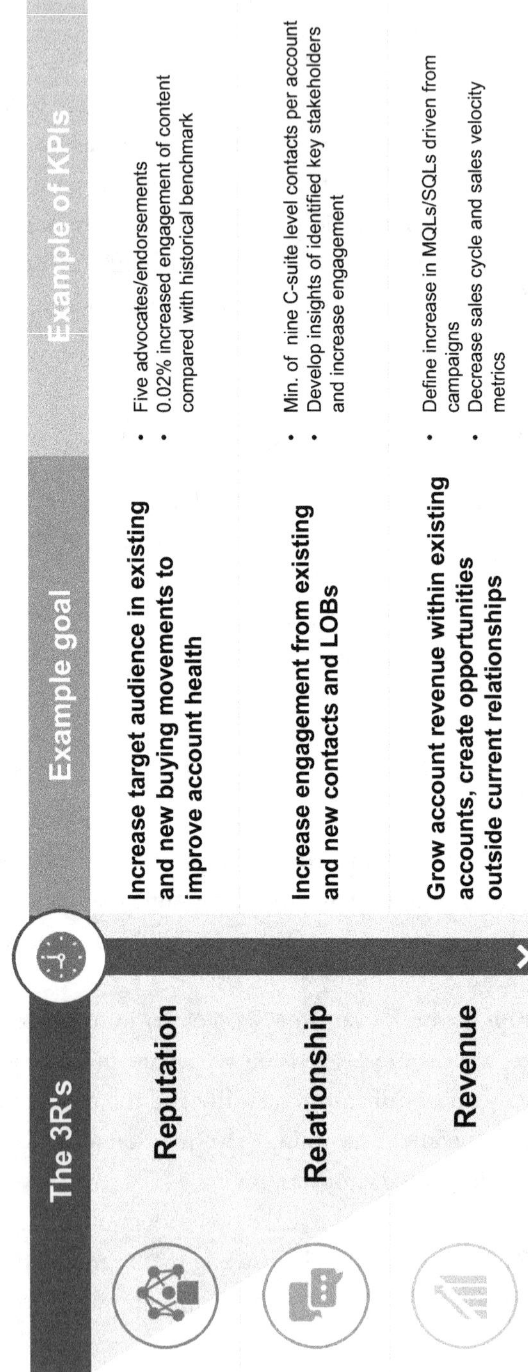

Figure 1.1 Three R's of ABM

dispel the notion that revenue is the most important indicator of long-term Strategic ABM success by asking the question: Are we impacting the pipeline and closed won business?

All three matter. And when properly taken and analyzed as a whole, they create a powerful story of progression. Let's break these down.

Reputation

What we measure:

- Brand sentiment within the account
- Positive mentions in meetings or industry events
- Share of voice versus competitors
- Executive awareness or familiarity with your firm
- Inclusion in requests for proposals (RFPs) or strategic conversations

A change in reputation is often the **first signal** that your ABM is working—even before a meeting is booked. We will discuss how we can capture trends and intent to help identify and quickly react to potential leads.

Relationship

How we measure:

- Number of net new stakeholder connections
- Engagement from VP+ roles or economic buyers
- Invitations to workshops or joint planning sessions
- Increased multithreading across buying units
- Internal account team's assessment of access level

Track this over time. Relationships are built slowly, but they're your most valuable asset.

Revenue

Where we measure:

- Influence on pipeline creation
- Acceleration of existing opportunities
- Expansion deals with current customers
- Win rate improvement
- Deal size and multiyear contract growth

Finally, why we measure:

While revenue is the most visible metric that we can measure, **ABM is not always a direct attribution game.** Sometimes your work is one of many influences. That's OK, as long as you can show causation and correlation.

Now that we've covered some simple background of what makes ABM different, we need to understand the three traditional types of ABM.

CHAPTER 2

The Strategic Pivot to 1:1 ABM

Pivoting isn't plan B; it's part of the process.

Jeff Goins[4]

An Introduction to Strategic ABM

Think about the messages that genuinely capture your attention—not the ones sent to everyone but the ones that speak directly to your situation. This level of focused communication is at the heart of Strategic ABM, often called 1:1 ABM by marketers in the field. It represents a shift from targeting a broad audience to concentrating intense effort on a single, high-value client, viewing them not just as a customer but as a unique market in themselves. Think about the 20 percent of your clients that tend to make up 80 percent of your annual revenue.

Implementing Strategic ABM requires truly paying attention to a your target accounts and committing marketing's time. It means investing time and effort to gain a deep understanding of each individual account's specific needs, pain points, and aspirations through careful investigation. Strategic ABM calls for crafting truly personalized experiences, moving far beyond generalized outreach, to create specific messages and interactions. To achieve this effectively requires sales and marketing teams to work closely together, ensuring a consistent and exceptional experience developed specifically for that one account. This focused, personalized approach helps build strong, lasting partnerships that benefit both parties. Evan Jordan, a colleague that is also a Strategic ABMer likes to say that it is about doing what is right for the client, even if that doesn't always align with the ambitions of the organization.

---

[4]Goins (2015).

What Is Strategic ABM?

We've all felt like just another number, right? Scrolling through endless generic messages, wading through marketing noise that clearly wasn't meant for us. Now, flip that around. Think about the times a message truly spoke to you, addressed something specific you were thinking about, perhaps even anticipated a need you didn't realize you had yet. That's a different feeling entirely. It feels personal. It feels like they get it.

Matthew Dixon, in *The Challenger Sale: Taking Control of the Customer Conversation* says, "But what if customers truly don't know what they need? What if customers' single greatest need—ironically—is to figure out exactly what they need?" **That is what Strategic ABM is meant to help the account team to accomplish.**

That feeling, scaled up and focused intently on the most valuable clients your business has, is the core idea behind what we call Strategic ABM or 1:1 ABM. Think of it not as marketing to a market, but marketing as a market. Each high-value client isn't just a dot on a spreadsheet; they are their own unique universe of needs, objectives, and ways of working. This approach means diving deep into what makes them tick, what challenges they face, and what they hope to achieve. It's also about working with an account team that isn't afraid to go with you on this journey and act as your navigator. The account team's job is to be there to tell you when you are off course and how to correct that course to ensure success for the entire team.

What makes this one-on-one approach stand out? It's the sheer dedication to making everything customized.

- It means crafting campaigns designed precisely for one account, not a hundred.
- It involves creating unique content and messages built around what that single account needs and wants.
- And yes, it demands putting in the work—significant effort in researching and customizing everything to fit their exact situation.
- The rewards for this level of focused effort are considerable.
- It helps build lasting working relationships, where both sides benefit over time.

- It ensures that everyone on your side, from sales to marketing, is working together to give the client a consistent, joined-up experience.
- It provides an experience crafted just for them, standing in clear contrast to more general marketing efforts.

Putting Strategic ABM into action isn't a small undertaking. It definitely calls for substantial effort in understanding and customization.

- This means doing thorough investigations to really grasp what each account is trying to do and what they need.
- You must build a clear picture of what makes each account distinct.
- Finally, it requires close cooperation between the sales and marketing teams to ensure the client's experience is unified. No more of the former generation's attitude toward sales. It's not them versus us. It's, we all row together, in the same direction, like the Navy SEALs. An old mentor of mine, Merlin Simpson, used to remind me of the importance of everyone working in unison. He would equate it to a symphony, and a beautiful one at that. "When we all come together and row in the same direction, there is nothing we cannot accomplish."

  To truly succeed with this kind of marketing, there are a few things to focus on.
  - Build that deep knowledge of what each account needs and wants. As well as the people who your account team wants to focus on and don't be afraid to ask, 'Why?'
  - Put together highly specific campaigns that connect directly with each account. This doesn't mean that you are creating one-off campaigns that cannot be lifted and shifted for other accounts.
  - Always measure what you're doing and keep adjusting your methods to improve results. I have yet to see a perfect way of measuring efforts in a quantitative manner for 1:1 ABM. Anyone who tells you that their platform or they themselves have the secret sauce, you should treat what they tell you with a good amount of skepticism. Working for seven years in home

> improvement advertising and marketing, I heard countless people come through our door telling me that they had this secret to increase close rates by over 30 percent. Whether it was Porch, Lowe's competitor to Angie's List, or a dozen other lead generation offerings, I always knew that their numbers were almost impossible to achieve, and in the end, they were.

Strategic ABM offers you a powerful way to stand out and succeed in today's competitive landscape. Adopting the Strategic ABM path allows for businesses to create a highly individualized marketing experience that connects deeply with individual accounts. This helps build strong, longterm connections that drives revenue growth. With its focus on investigation, customization, and cooperation, Strategic ABM enables you to move beyond campaigns and build meaningful, enduring relationships.

The Evolution of ABM and Its Tiers

At the start of my career, I used to just oversee sending out the mail to accounts and being the Napoleon's savant. This meant people would read copy to me to see if I understood the message then that means it was simple enough for anyone to comprehend. Eventually I got my very first campaign, overseeing a bicycle helmet safety campaign for children. I only got media coverage from one station and a handful of children to turn up to my event. It was the start of feeling like my marketing efforts felt like shouting into a vacuum. The real breakthrough, the shift that made marketing feel less like broadcasting and more like having a focused conversation, came from an evolved way of thinking about accounts.

We're going to need to go back a bit, and, honestly, the approach was almost artisanal. As a part of a business development team in London, I spent days, weeks even, researching a single company. We would dig deep, understand the decision makers, the challenges, the goals. Then, we'd spend a week or two crafting something utterly unique for just that one account—a piece of content, a presentation, an experience designed specifically for them. One time, I worked on a horrible idea to create the 'stages' of a woman's life in a boardroom. Basically, my boss wanted to create five or six different 'small stages' around the room to show a potential client that made feminine hygiene products that, 'we understood' what it meant to be a woman. If you're keeping score at home, we didn't win this pitch idea to P&G.

This was all the way back in 2007, only about three years after the term ABM was coined by Bev Burgess. And while our pitch turned out to be a flop, it was the first time I thought about highly personalized and targeted messaging. The idea focused on building strong connections because it showed genuine understanding and effort. And think about the effort involved in the pitch that I just mentioned. Each 'stage' was a custom build. It required significant investment of people's time and creative energy. You couldn't do this for hundreds or thousands of accounts. Consequently, this deep, one-to-one work was reserved for only the most strategically important potential customers, the ones where winning the business could genuinely move the needle for our company. While the idea was flawed in execution, it made me step back and think more strategically about our audiences.

During this time, businesses were aiming for broader market penetration and consistent growth. While B2B companies wanted to target decision makers, the limitations of this manual, highly individualized approach became apparent. Marketers needed a way to keep that valuable personalization but apply it more widely. The goal became finding a balance: how do you maintain tailored engagement without needing an army of marketers crafting bespoke messages for every single prospect? This pressure led to the development of different ways to apply ABM principles across varying groups of accounts.

What emerged is what is often referred to as the tiered ABM model. It provides a framework for applying ABM strategies with different levels of intensity, matching the effort to the potential return from different account segments.

At the top, for those few accounts that represent massive opportunities, is Strategic ABM, sometimes called 1:1 ABM by many practitioners. This is the direct descendant of that early, manual approach. It involves intensive research on individual accounts, highly personalized content, and direct, personal engagement from sales and marketing. This tier is about building deep, lasting ties with specific, high-value targets. It creates the highest potential rewards with the greatest risk. And what we're going to be focusing on in this book.

Moving down the triangle, you find ABM Lite, or 1:Few. This approach is for groups of accounts that share similar characteristics or challenges. You still apply personalization, but you do it for the segment rather than the individual account. Think targeted messaging campaigns, content relevant to that specific group, and scaled engagement strategies. It offers more efficiency than 1:1 while retaining personalization and some customization.

Finally, there's Programmatic ABM, also called the 1:Many tier. This utilizes technology and automation to reach larger groups of accounts based on data-driven insights. While less deeply personalized than the other tiers, it allows you to apply ABM principles like targeted advertising and scaled content distribution across many accounts efficiently. It's about using data and tech to personalize at scale for broader segments with collective potential. Think more verticalized messaging toward a subcategory. And the idea of the work done in 1:1 ABM is to trickle down learnings to Programmatic so the learnings can eventually be replicated at scale. This understanding is key to 1:1 ABM because you want to find a way to replicate your efforts, eventually, to the largest audience possible.

Choosing the correct tier hinges on your available resources—the size of your team, your budget, the martech stack you have access to—and the potential value each target account or segment represents. Evaluating your goals and understanding your target account landscape are essential steps. Selecting the approach that aligns with these factors allows you to focus your efforts where they'll be most impactful, driving better returns and contributing to sustainable growth. The journey of ABM has truly transformed it from a specialized, labor-intensive tactic into an adaptable strategy businesses can use to engage accounts based on their unique value and characteristics.

While I'm particular to utilizing a 1:1 ABM approach when starting the journey because it tends to show the greatest return and creates better communication across marketing and sales, there is no one model fits all. It depends on your resources, your offerings, the relationships that your account teams already have in place, and the organization's faith in developing a full end-to-end ABM offering. I've seen great success with starting at ABM Lite and creating multiple campaigns with 15 to 20 accounts per each region. And then monitoring those campaigns and when specific accounts showed significant intent then transferring those accounts into 1:1 campaigns.

Distinguishing 1:1 from 1:Few and 1:Many

Anyone who has ever tried to achieve something significant knows that scattering your energy rarely yields the best outcome. Whether you're trying to build a strong relationship, master a skill, or outthink your opponent, focusing your efforts on a precise target tends to produce more impactful results. That is why it's important to understand the pros and cons of each tactic in your ABM arsenal. Much like fencing, where you have three weapons, beginner fencers rarely focus on more than one weapon.

ABM isn't just a marketing tactic, it's a strategic pivot. It's about identifying the accounts that matter most to the organization and then approaching them with campaigns and messages crafted specifically for their unique context. It means having meaningful conversations with someone you truly want to connect with. This strategic focus isn't monolithic; it manifests in three main ways, each requiring a different level of intensity and resource dedication: Strategic or 1:1 ABM, ABM Lite or 1:Few, and Programmatic or 1:Many ABM. They differ in how much personalization is applied, the resources needed, and the size and nature of the target group (Figure 2.1).

Strategic or 1:1 ABM

> *Sloan was instrumental in designing bespoke campaigns for one of my largest accounts. These were not your typical high-touch campaigns. These were carefully targeted messages that not only led to client interest in expanding our current footprint, but it also helped generate a face-to-face executive positioning meeting with our key client stakeholders.*
>
> Kyle McGrotty, Senior Client Manager at NTT Ltd

Strategic 1:1 ABM represents the pinnacle of this focused strategy. Here, the effort is concentrated on individual accounts, crafting highly customized experiences for the individuals who hold sway within them. This calls

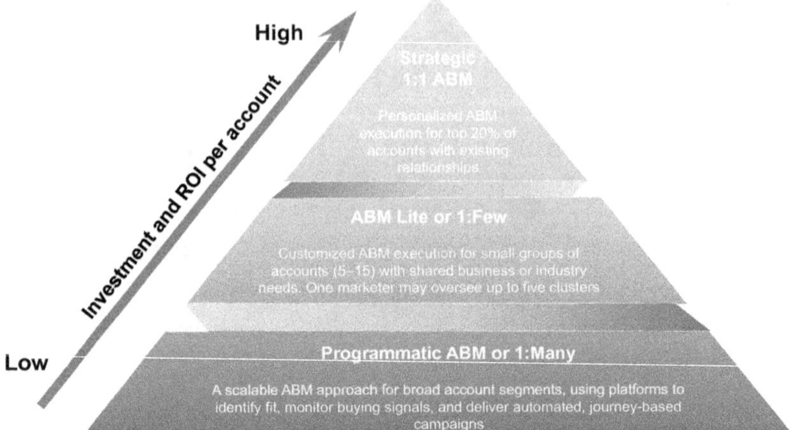

Figure 2.1 Types of ABM and with investment/ROI

for significant resources poured into each account. The goal is to co-create value propositions that speak directly to the priorities, hurdles, and aspirations of the key figures you're trying to reach. The messages are entirely custom, not standard templates. Getting this right means having a very clear understanding of each account's specific requirements and objectives. This is the stage where you truly embed yourself with account teams. Where you will have salespeople begging to be placed on ABM 1:1 campaigns, if done properly.

Consider a situation where a company used A/B testing for e-mail outreach as part of their Strategic ABM efforts. They discovered their normal e-mails, formatted with HTML, were being blocked by a client's security measures, leading to virtually no opens (less than 1 percent). By adapting and sending simpler, less elaborately designed e-mails, they saw open rates jump by 44 percent and achieve a click-through rate exceeding 60 percent. These figures are much higher than typical B2B e-mail benchmarks, which usually hover between 15 to 25 percent for opens and 2 to 5 percent for clicks. This simple change, driven by understanding a specific account's technical reality, shows the power of tailoring the approach.

ABM Lite or 1:1 Few

Moving down the ABM Triangle, ABM Lite or 1:Few ABM focuses on groups or clusters of accounts that share similar characteristics or needs.

Messaging is still customized, but it's adapted for the shared requirements of the cluster, rather than being unique for each single account. This approach requires less resource investment per account than Strategic ABM but still involves a notable degree of personalization. It allows companies to create effective campaigns by addressing commonalities within specific segments.

Programmatic or 1:1 Many ABM

At the base of the ABM Triangle is Programmatic or 1:Many ABM. This is the most generalized, scaled marketing stance, applying broader messaging across a larger group of potential accounts. In many cases when you here vendors like Demandbase or 6sense discuss their ABM platforms, this is how they tend to define ABM. It's often used when there are many potential targets and resources are constrained. While not as deeply personal as the other two methods, 1:Many can be an effective way to engage a larger pool of accounts and monitor intent. If you are a new company with new offerings and you've not fully cultivated your audience and building your CRM database, then this could be a great way to begin your journey.

Naturally, how you allocate resources varies considerably across these three approaches. Strategic ABM demands a substantial investment per account, requiring customized messaging, tailored content, and campaigns built from the ground-up for that specific target. Essentially, the biggest investment for the biggest reward. 1:Few and 1:Many ABM are less resource-intensive on a per-account basis because they use more personalized messages and fewer fully personalized campaigns.

Understanding these distinctions helps companies select the method that aligns best with their specific aims, available resources, and the audience they wish to reach. Whether the strategy involves crafting hyperpersonalized interactions for a few key figures or using broader communication for a wider set of accounts, ABM provides a range of pathways for companies to connect with their desired accounts and stimulate growth.

Now that we've defined how these three tiers differ, let's dive into Strategic ABM.

The Strategic Imperative for High-Value Accounts

In the world of business growth, not all accounts are made equal. Some accounts stand out, promising a return on your time and resources that far exceeds the average account. Recognizing and nurturing these select few accounts aren't just smart; it's the core concept behind Strategic ABM.

Think about the accounts that could truly move the needle for your organization. These are the ones capable of generating substantial income. Their value often stems from factors like their sheer size, their standing within their industry, or how well their objectives match your organization's direction. Pinpointing these accounts requires looking closely at your target market—understanding things like company size, revenue figures, their industry, and the steps they take when making purchasing decisions. By focusing your view on key accounts, you ensure your marketing efforts are pointed directly where they matter most, making your investment work as efficiently as possible to produce the best outcome.

Once you've identified your target accounts, treating them with a one-size-fits-all approach just doesn't make sense. Building solid, enduring connections with them calls for experiences crafted specifically for them. This means taking the time to really understand what drives each account—their unique needs, the specific hurdles they face. When you can offer solutions designed to address their needs, you build trust and encourage continued relationship growth. This personalized way of working helps you stand apart from others, showing a dedication to providing exceptional service and paying close attention to detail.

Growing up around PR professionals, I saw firsthand what it meant to truly know your clients. My father maintained detailed notes on every key stakeholder—tracking anniversaries, children's birthdays, and personal milestones. He would send flowers or thoughtful gifts to mark these occasions, not as a tactic, but as a genuine gesture of care. It was a level of personalization and relationship-building that's rare in our industry today—and one I still draw inspiration from. This way of building relationships is the cornerstone of Strategic ABM.

Knowing the individual needs of each account is vital for directing your overall strategy and getting the best return on your investment. Your account team usually knows this, but the marketing department is usually in the dark, when it comes to specific accounts. When your marketing actions line-up with specific aims and goals of each high-value account, you ensure that your plans are relevant, work effectively, and that you can track that success.

Providing truly exceptional service to these accounts often means having dedicated teams assigned to them. These teams are consist of skilled professionals who deeply grasp the account's requirements and aspirations. They are tasked with providing support tailored to the account, handling any concerns that arise, and identifying opportunities for further engagement and expansion. Investing in these dedicated teams guarantees that your most valuable accounts receive the focus and high level of service they deserve. This builds loyalty, keeps them around longer, and contributes to revenue growth. As a Strategic ABM practitioner or ABMer, you should be able to command the attention and respect of these skilled professionals.

Directing your 1:1 ABM strategy toward these high-value accounts allows you to concentrate your efforts where they can yield significant returns. This approach helps you:

- Drive more revenue from these important customers.
- Build stronger, lasting working relationships.
- Develop long-standing partnerships with potential vendors.
- Increases how long accounts stay with your business.
- Get the best ROI from your marketing investment.

Realizing this and having the confidence to take action is the first step in becoming the CMO of your 1:1 ABM accounts. A term commonly used to describe how 1:1 ABMers see themselves.

Setting the Stage for White-Glove Treatment

All tiers of ABM are about treating each account, each potential partner, as its own unique world—a market unto itself. Getting this right demands dedicated effort to truly grasp what makes your account's world turn. It means going beyond surface-level details, digging deep through research to uncover their specific obstacles, their ambitions, and their unique landscape. When you invest the time to gather these insights—understanding their particular needs, the pain points that keep them up at night, and the goals they are striving for—you gain the perspective needed to shape your approach. You can then craft strategies that feel purpose-built, speaking directly to the individuals who make the critical choices.

Strategic ABM is the most precise of all the ABM efforts. In many ways, the Strategic ABMer is the surgeon of modern marketing.

Why Personalization Is Essential

You can't automate insight. You can't outsource trust. And it's impossible for you to fake personalization.

Personalization signifies a deliberate move away from broad, mainstream messaging and content. Instead, the focus shifts to delivering communications and experiences that are precisely targeted and relevant, directly addressing what each specific account requires. Studies have consistently indicated that marketing efforts infused with this level of personalization are significantly more effective at driving initial interest, motivating people toward action, and ultimately contributing to growth.

To genuinely provide outstanding value, it's necessary for sales and marketing teams to operate in unison. It's important that you can embed yourself with the account team. Having a shared purpose should be clear: delivering experiences that are customized to meet the distinct requirements of each account. This calls for tight coordination, consistent dialogue, and a mutual understanding of the account's objectives and challenges. I find that managing a weekly call with each account team is key to accomplishing this outcome. By operating as a single unit, we ensure that stakeholders receive attentive, highly personal content and service—a level of support that anticipates needs and proactively addresses potential issues before they even surface.

Elements of Effective Teamwork

Making sure sales and marketing work together effectively involves several fundamental components:

- **Consistent Dialogue:** Regular, transparent communication is necessary to ensure that both teams are synchronized and pursuing the same objectives. Don't be afraid to constantly ask questions during this dialogue. That means you need to be the ambassador of ABM.
- **Shared Aspirations:** Sales and marketing teams must possess a common understanding of the account's aspirations and the methods for achieving them. Over time a Strategic ABMer may become more closely aligned with the account team and become critical of traditional marketing tactics.
- **Clear Responsibilities:** Defining roles and responsibilities clearly helps avoid confusion, duplicate work, and ensures that each team operates efficiently.

Providing this elevated level of support, often described as white-glove service, is about offering proactive, customized help that foresees and resolves potential problems before they arise. You can only accomplish this level of attention via a thorough understanding of the account's requirements and a commitment to delivering considerable value. Offering white-glove service will lead to increased businesses confidence, establish enduring connections, build trust and foster growth. One of the best compliments I ever received came from a client stakeholder who said, "This feels like you're inside our company." That's what all Strategic ABMers should aim for: creating a sense of being side-by-side with your target account.

My Journey to White- Glove Experiences

I'll admit it—I've always been drawn to the idea of personalized experiences. Back in university, I remember reading about a Coca-Cola campaign that used real-time customer data to personalize messages on a bridge. It captured my imagination. A decade later, I found myself drawing on that same inspiration when I launched an award-winning social campaign that put one lucky participant in a Patriot Jet during Seattle's Seafair event.

Customization Isn't Just Clever—It Connects

Real connection goes far beyond clever campaigns or surface-level customization. It means recognizing that people don't buy the same way—and that meaningful engagement starts with understanding. Truly effective ABM, especially 1:1, demands we move past generalized strategies and focus on the nuanced ways individuals and organizations make decisions.

I've seen this firsthand across different markets and regions. Working with businesses taught me the complexity of buying groups and the importance of tailoring programs to measurable outcomes. Serving individual consumers underscored the need for emotional resonance and lifestyle alignment. Direct-to-consumer (D2C) service showed me the value of trust and delivering consistent, personalized experiences. In Europe, I learned the importance of localization and cultural nuance, while North America emphasized high-velocity growth paired with account-specific precision.

One project still stands out: while building a global website for ATE brake fluids, we hit a wall with the Brazil team. They wouldn't approve our messaging. It wasn't until I sat down with them that I uncovered the real issue—they didn't sell all the global products we were showcasing. By listening first, we were able to adjust the platform to reflect their reality. The issue wasn't resistance—it was misalignment. Once we understood that, the solution came quickly.

Early on, I relied on broad messaging, thinking that a polished message could scale. But I quickly learned the limits of that way of thinking. Engagement doesn't come from broadcasting; it comes from relevance. And relevance requires deep research, tailored value propositions, and intentional storytelling.

This journey shaped how I approach 1:1 ABM: identifying high-impact accounts, understanding the people within them, uncovering their pain points, and crafting messages that resonate. It's about aligning marketing with sales, targeting outreach at the individual level, and measuring success with metrics that matter. Personalization isn't just a strategy—it's a discipline. And it's worth the effort.

Recognizing the Need for Deep Personalization in Business

Reaching the accounts that matter most feels different. It's not spray and pray; it's surgical precision. For many who are first dipping their toes into ABM, this distinction will quickly become apparent. Simply slapping a company name on an e-mail won't be enough. Those initial attempts at ABM often highlight a fundamental truth: treating every target account the same way yields disappointing returns and low ROI.

Consider the messaging. ABM efforts in the early 2000s frequently used approaches barely different from mass marketing. The communication wasn't truly built for a specific recipient. This disconnect meant that customized messages often fell flat. Engagement suffered. You might send out a beautifully designed HTML e-mail, only to discover that client's firewalls were blocking it entirely, leading to open rates dipping below 0.5 percent. This lack of basic tailoring, let alone deeper understanding, demonstrated the clear limitations of a one-size-fits-all approach. When I first joined the ABM division, I noticed this exact issue. We had an account that we were onboarding and were using traditional lead generation marketing tactics that were failing to even get close to the senior leadership we targeted. After the first round of failed e-mails, I created A/B testing for a staggered e-mail nurture campaign that we were able to have sent out as it was coming from the Client Executive. Thanks to our marketing automation platform, we were able to create a more honest and personalized message and track everything back into our CRM. This allowed for not only real-time analysis but to convey to the account team any client engagement allowing them to immediately reach out to the account. A trick that I'd learned from working with Salesforce.

As I experimented and learned, the path forward became clearer. Genuine connection with important accounts demanded a deeper understanding their unique business situation. This isn't guesswork; it comes from dedicated investigation into the specific needs and intricacies of each potential customer. I was one of the first Strategic ABM marketers to be invited to sit down and present our ABM campaigns directly to executive client stakeholders to ensure that our messaging was on target. If you're able to find an advocate within your target account and you don't take advantage of them, then you're wasting a golden opportunity (Figure 2.2).

When you show a true willingness to discuss and address your Strategic ABM account's particular circumstances, you build trust and make your value proposition undeniable. Data backs this up: a strong commitment to personalization has been shown to improve open rates by 44 percent and click-through rates by 70 percent.

The ultimate aim of your strategy needs to make your target account trust you more and want to work with you on additional opportunities.

My father always told me that when someone is 'good' at PR, people know their name. But when you're 'great' at it, then people won't even know you did anything. It's kind of like that quote from Charles Baudelaire, "The greatest trick the devil ever pulled was convincing the world he didn't exist." That's the same thing with great Strategic ABM campaigns. It looks like, to the client that this is just how you treat every account.

To accomplish this, it means shifting away from mass communication and toward providing value tailored specifically for one account at a time. This demands a change in perspective, moving focus from simply reaching many to making a significant impact on a select few. By directing resources toward high-potential accounts and delivering content that is truly relevant to them, marketing becomes a clear driver of business results, proving its financial impact. Even though you may begin building these campaigns for one account at a time, eventually you will find overlaps and the ability to 'lift and shift' efforts across from Strategic ABM downstream and eventually to your Programmatic ABM efforts.

The financial upside in Strategic ABM doesn't come from reaching vast numbers. It arises from focused effort and accuracy. By putting resources into understanding individual accounts and crafting specific value propositions, marketers can generate substantial returns. Compared to broader marketing efforts, Strategic ABM has consistently shown superior results, making it a compelling strategy for companies looking to achieve growth and revenue with their most valuable customers. And that means committing a marketer to 10 to 24 months of being embedded with a target account.

Shifting Focus to Strategic Account Engagement

Moving from broad, traditional view of marketing to Strategic ABM, requires what amounts to a mindset transformation. Marketing is no longer merely tactical; it has finally evolved into being a strategic redirection that places the most important customers—your high-value accounts—squarely at the center of all go-to-market activities. This kind of change touches the very fiber of an organization, demanding that teams typically operating in silos, like sales, marketing, and those focused on customer experience, begin working together in a far more connected and unified fashion.

Consider the core difference. Traditional marketing aims for mass outreach, focused on filling a funnel with leads. Strategic ABM, by contrast, zeros in on engaging specific, high-value accounts and the key individuals within them. This distinct approach necessitates a different calculation for marketers when it comes to how resources are spent, what kind of content is developed, and how success is ultimately measured. In a traditional structure, marketing might feel separate from sales operations. Under an ABM model, marketing becomes a true peer, collaborating side by side with sales, dedicated to driving account growth and building lasting customer loyalty.

Making this switch successfully hinges on cultivating certain ways of thinking. Several elements are critical for this shift to Strategic ABM to take root:

- **Customer-centricity:** Placing the customer experience and needs at the very heart of every action taken by go-to-market teams.
- **Collaboration:** Fostering strong working relationships across sales, marketing, and customer experience departments.

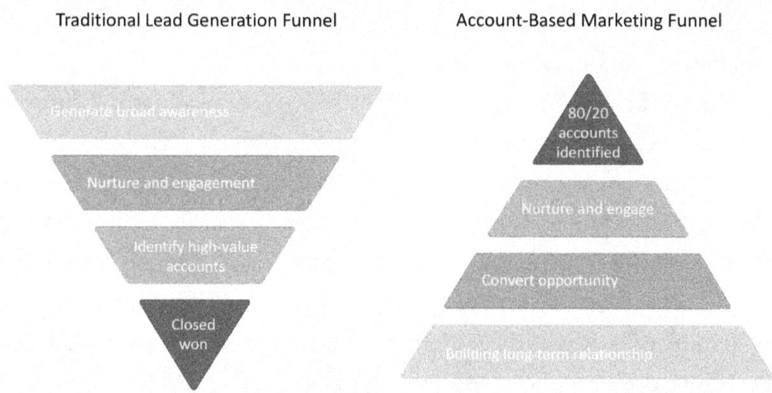

Figure 2.2 Lead Gen funnel versus ABM funnel

- **Targeted engagement:** Directing efforts specifically toward high-value accounts and the relevant individuals within them, moving away from broad campaigns.
- **Personalization:** Crafting messaging and content that speaks directly to the specific needs and context of target accounts.
- **Measurement:** Utilizing both data-driven insights and qualitative feedback to gauge account interaction and overall success.

Adopting Strategic ABM isn't without its hurdles. It can present significant challenges, particularly for organizations deeply rooted in traditional marketing practices and established workflows. Yet the opportunities that lie on the other side of this transition are substantial and far outweigh the difficulties. This includes the chance to increase account growth and strengthen customer loyalty by building deeper, more meaningful connections with those key customers. It also offers the potential to significantly improve alignment between sales and marketing teams, as they work collaboratively toward shared goals of account engagement and expansion.

Early Experiments and My Learnings in ABM 1:1

Starting out with 1:1 ABM often feels like venturing into new territory, bringing both possibility and uncertainty. For us, this meant beginning small, applying 1:1 ABM principles to a limited set of targeted strategic accounts. This measured start let us test the waters, refine our approach, and gradually build momentum.

One of the earliest and most important lessons was getting support from the top. Without leadership backing, securing necessary resources—the right team, the needed budget—proved difficult. Having someone have my back was key. It meant we could assemble dedicated teams and secure the budget required to run our campaigns. On my first week I would meet Matt Preschern, then the CMO of NTT Ltd, and he told me to think of myself as the CMO of my accounts. This is something that I still do to this day whenever I work with any account.

With leaders behind you, you can prioritize your efforts, focusing on high-potential accounts and measuring results precisely.

Another lesson was something that I've talked about over and over, the importance of personalization. Generic messaging, even slightly tweaked, didn't land well. In contrast, content and experiences made specifically for target accounts, showing we understood their business needs and issues, worked much better. Making time to sit down and talk to account stakeholders on the client side. This showed me the importance of removing accounts from generic marketing messaging to help ensure their specific needs didn't appear to be ignored.

And a great way to make someone feel heard is with quality data. Data isn't just a tool; it's foundational. Poor or incomplete data makes it almost impossible to personalize, leading to missed chances and less campaign success. Good data allowed us to create targeted, relevant content that spoke directly to their needs and concerns, making efforts far more effective.

Figuring out if our 1:1 ABM efforts were working meant using new ways to measure, specific to each account. We had to shift our mindset. Standard marketing numbers, like lead volume, didn't tell the whole story. Instead, we focused on numbers showing the depth of our connections: how much of the account we touched, how much they engaged, and revenue growth.

Through our early tries with 1:1 ABM, we saw that constantly tweaking and improving was necessary to truly connect with important accounts. This was an ongoing process. Keeping a close watch and adapting let us make our methods better over time, handling issues and taking chances as they appeared.

There are many more lessons that we're going to discuss but with support, personalization and good data. You can figure the rest out.

The Power of Mentorship and Trusted Partners

I'd be remiss not to talk about the importance of having the right mentors and partners alongside you. Strategic ABM can be incredibly rewarding—but also lonely, vulnerable work. You're often navigating competing priorities from leadership, sales, and marketing while trying to change how your organization shows up to its most important clients.

That's why you need people who ground you. People who remind you of your strategy when the noise gets loud. People who challenge your thinking and have your back when things get messy. For me, that person was Gayle Duffy, former Director of CoE ABM at NTT Ltd.

She was my mentor, sounding board, and the "woman in the chair." No matter how chaotic things got—or how off course I felt—Gayle believed in me. Even now, years later, when I'm wrestling with a complex account or trying to decide on the next step, I'll reach out to her. And somehow, she always helps me to find my way through it.

I believe almost any experienced marketer can develop a successful ABM program—but it's a whole lot easier, and far more fulfilling, when you have great people in your corner.

And you cannot forget the frontline: the account team. ABM requires significant, dedicated involvement from sales members who must actively participate in account-specific strategies. Do they have the availability to commit time and resources to these initiatives? Do they possess the account-specific knowledge required? Can they actively engage with targets and execute those tailored strategies?

By finding the right people to have in your corner, you will go from constantly being overwhelmed to being able to approach any account with the necessary confidence to be successful in this space.

How Does Agentic AI Fit into All of This?

Agentic AI is no longer an abstract concept or futuristic buzzword confined to the walls of research labs and Silicon Valley conferences. It has entered the mainstream—quietly, but profoundly—reshaping how we live, work, and make decisions. Today, it sits at the intersection of technology and human intention, influencing industries from healthcare and finance to education and marketing.

At its core, **Agentic AI** refers to systems capable of acting autonomously to pursue defined goals. These are not simply tools awaiting instructions. They interpret, analyze, decide, and execute—continually refining their performance through learning. They are, in essence, digital collaborators that think and act with a level of independence once reserved for humans.

In the world of **Account-Based Marketing**, this development represents one of the most transformative shifts in a generation. ABM has always demanded an intricate balance between art and science—between data-driven insight and human connection. Agentic AI brings both dimensions closer together, enabling personalization at a level of precision and scale we could only dream of a few years ago.

The Daily Transformation of ABM

The work of an ABM leader is rarely glamorous. It involves hours spent aligning data, building account dossiers, interpreting buying signals, and ensuring that every piece of content lands with relevance. Agentic AI transforms this routine. It steps into the background to automate the repetitive, synthesize the complex, and surface what matters most.

- **Account Research Agents** can now scan thousands of public and proprietary sources to produce concise, account-specific summaries—highlighting strategic priorities, leadership shifts, and emerging opportunities.
- **Engagement Monitoring Agents** track stakeholder behavior across multiple platforms, alerting marketing and sales teams when engagement drops, or new intent appears.
- **Content Optimization Agents** continuously analyze creative and performance data to recommend iterations that increase resonance, tailoring not only the message but the moment of delivery.
- **Relationship Agents** monitor CRM updates, meeting notes, and social signals to detect when a stakeholder goes silent, or a new decision maker enters the scene—prompting timely, meaningful outreach.

This is not theoretical. These use cases are already being piloted across industries, including my own experiences working with Salesforce's Agentforce ecosystem. When I earned my **Salesforce Agentic AI Certification**, it wasn't just about acquiring another technical credential—it was about reimagining how we work. Agentic AI isn't here to replace marketers. It's here to *free* them.

From Manual Personalization to Predictive Precision

For years, personalization in ABM depended on human intuition: connecting disparate signals, crafting tailored messages, and mapping the emotional texture of a relationship. That human instinct remains irreplaceable. But now, it can be **augmented by precision**. Agentic systems continuously learn from data, evolving to predict which accounts are most likely to engage, which relationships are at risk, and which creative approaches are gaining traction within a buying group.

In my early years leading Strategic ABM, I saw the consequences of imperfect account selection firsthand. Nearly 40 percent of the accounts we attempted to onboard didn't make it through the first year—usually because of hidden misalignments that weren't evident at the outset. An agentic ABM agent, trained on selection criteria and historical success factors, could have analyzed firmographic, technographic, and behavioral variables to flag those risks in advance. The potential impact is not just efficiency—it's precision empathy.

The Human Element Remains the Core

The great misunderstanding about AI—gen, agentic, or otherwise—is that it removes the human from the equation. The reality is the opposite. By automating the mechanical, it magnifies the creative. It gives Strategic ABMers the gift of time: to think, to connect, to tell better stories, and to cocreate value with clients.

I often describe it as a new kind of partnership—a *copilot* dynamic where AI manages the turbulence of data and logistics, while humans steer the emotional and relational course. Agentic AI doesn't diminish our role; it deepens it. It allows marketers to focus on what technology still cannot replicate: trust, intuition, empathy, and narrative.

A New Era of Precision Empathy

As we stand at the edge of this next evolution, the promise of Agentic AI extends far beyond efficiency. It offers a way to merge analytics with artistry, allowing personalization to become truly dynamic—shifting and evolving in rhythm with each account relationship. It represents a movement toward what I call *precision empathy*—where every interaction is informed by intelligence but shaped by human understanding.

This, to me, is where the future of ABM becomes exciting. Agentic AI is not a shortcut. It's a multiplier. It's the quiet force that enables Strategic ABMers to lead with foresight, to operate with greater agility, and to elevate personalization from a task into an art form.

I'm not apprehensive about this evolution. I'm energized by it. Agentic AI isn't merely reshaping how we work—it's redefining what's possible for those willing to embrace it early, experiment boldly, and lead with vision.

CHAPTER 3

Designing the Bespoke Experience

There's never nothing going on. There are no ordinary moments.
Dan Millman, Way of the Peaceful Warrior[5]

Strategic Messaging ≠ Campaign Slogans

We are all very aware that the current business environment is a typhoon of information and competition. Companies face the constant challenge of being heard and building meaningful connections amidst overwhelming noise. In our reality, simply having a groundbreaking product or service is not enough.

Cutting through all the clutter requires relevance. Generic, one-size-fits-all approaches are easily dismissed by today's buyers, who are bombarded with countless messages. And at the end of the day there is a cost-saving mentality of many companies based on decades-old attitudes toward how marketing works. But in many of today's B2B environments, Demand Generation and other traditional marketing practices are no longer yielding the ROI they once did.[6] Trying to get a decision maker to take a second look at your product when you're showing the CEO of a company the same message that you show to the first-year employee no longer resonates to get you new opportunities. The basic personalization from marketing automation platforms is quickly dismissed by C-suite executives and/or key stakeholders. People expect organizations to show they are understanding their unique challenges and specific goals. This expectation transforms relevance from a preference into a fundamental requirement for being successful.

Customization is the powerful method that makes relevance possible. It demonstrates that your audience is seen and heard by you and

---

[5]Millman (1980).
[6]Singh (2025).

your organization. It reinforces that your organization has a deeper understanding and provides real value by tailoring interactions based on data and insights. This approach doesn't just feel better; it builds trust, drives engagement, and produces concrete business results. I once worked at a service company that had an outdated Field Service Management platform with an automation progress tool. You would get an update when a product arrived at the warehouse and when it was ready to be installed. It was a wonderful tool for customer visibility on higher dollar home improvement projects. I took that tool and inserted additional marketing messaging to help cross-sell already existing clients on additional improvements and ideas for their home by just adding relevant services into this platform. It was a simple project that increased return business from this audience by 2.5 percent during the first four months. By just identifying what work the customer had done and then creating some messaging to drop in that was common with whatever repair or upgrade that we were doing, allowed for us to create a slightly personalized message to our existing customer base and provide warm leads for our field sales team.

The Demand for Relevance in Modern Business Relationships

Walk into almost any business today, and you'll sense it immediately. A hum, perhaps, or maybe just a feeling of being adrift in a sea of activity. Businesses are facing more complexity and more competitors daily. There simply so many asks to organizations—information, possibilities, demands—that figuring out how to be heard, how to connect with the people you want to reach, feels overwhelming. But look closer, and you'll see something cutting through that chaos: relevance. It's the way businesses can navigate the noise and build relationships that will lead to more opportunities. And in the proper culture, Strategic ABM managers can act with agility to help account teams make those connections.

Think about it. Relevance isn't optional anymore. With endless digital avenues and social feeds constantly vying for attention, buyers are drowning in generic messages, ads, and content that feels utterly impersonal.

This has made them far more selective. Clients expect you, the vendor, to grasp their specific challenges and objectives. Research backs this up; buyers are more inclined to interact with brands that show they genuinely understand their unique difficulties and goals.

Broad, generalized marketing and sales strategies simply don't cut it anymore. In a crowded marketplace where everyone is fighting for attention, the only approach that breaks through is one that's focused, personal, and deeply relevant. The old "one-size-fits-all" approach is outdated because buyers seek vendors who can offer customized insights and solutions that directly address their specific needs.

This becomes even more critical in Strategic ABM, especially when you're working with global accounts. Messaging that resonates in North America may fall flat in Europe or Asia. Cultural context, business norms, and stakeholder priorities differ—sometimes dramatically. What works in one region may need to be completely rethought for another. Precision matters. And so does relevance.

This is where personalization shows its strength. It's a powerful way to demonstrate real understanding and provide value, which builds confidence and believability with buyers. By using information and insights wisely, businesses can craft personal experiences that boost engagement, lead to more conversions, and ultimately, drive revenue growth.

What powers these meaningful interactions? Data and insights. They are the fuel for relevance. By using data analysis effectively, businesses can gain a clearer picture of what their customers need, prefer, and how they behave. This understanding then allows for the creation of specific content, offers, and experiences that genuinely resonate with the target audience.

The advantages of focusing on relevance are clear and widespread. Increased engagement is a major one; personal experiences lead to higher engagement and conversions, which means more revenue. Relevance also builds trust, leading to stronger, more significant connections with customers. And finally, businesses that prioritize relevance gain a real competitive advantage. They stand out from rivals and can become thought leaders into their target accounts.

Building Trust and Rapport with Key Decision Makers

In the highly meticulous world of Strategic ABM, where one of the three R's of ABM is forging strong connections with specific, high-value accounts or **relationships** there's a fundamental element that makes everything work. It's not about fancy tactics or cutting-edge technology; it's about something far more human: **trust and the easy understanding that comes with it.** Think of it as the bedrock. Without it, the entire structure of a potential partnership feels shaky. It's what allows businesses to build deep, lasting ties with the companies they most want to work alongside to develop long-term relationships. I'm going to now lay out why this foundation matters so much in Strategic ABM and share practical ways to establish and care for these vital connections.

To truly build that sense of trust and ease of understanding, you first must step into the world of the people you're talking to. Specifically, the decision makers. What keeps them up at night? What wins are they chasing? You need to understand their individual priorities. You need to be very perceptive of the world around you. This is a highbrow way of saying, always be learning. Accomplishing this means looking past surface-level details and getting to grips with a company's big-picture goals, the specific difficulties they face, and what truly drives them professionally. When you invest the time to dig in and understand their unique situation, you can shape what you say in a way that truly speaks to them. It shows that you've done your homework and that you care about what they're trying to accomplish.

I'm not saying you need to understand everything about your target audiences all the way back to grade school, but it has proven helpful to realize things like that 60 percent of the senior leadership team attended the same business school. And then selecting an executive sponsor who also attended that same school or a rival school. It creates underlying icebreakers to help set yourself up for success.

Data and insights aren't just a nice-to-have; they are key for building out relationships. You show this by connecting the dots between the target audience, their needs and how your product or service helps them get there. When you clearly demonstrate the practical benefits and the value your solution brings to their organization, you start to become more than just a vendor. You become a thought leader, a true collaborator, a partner.

Being real and open in these conversations matters immensely. Honesty builds belief and deepens the relationship.

So, how do you put this into practice? Several straightforward methods can help you build trust and understanding with the people who make decisions:

- **Speak their language:** Keep your communication tailored specifically to them. Regular, relevant conversations help build familiarity and make connections stronger. I can't reinforce this enough. If you don't have experience writing to a multitude of audiences, then you will put your foot in your mouth with your selected account. If your messages don't resonate with them then all of your work and investment will be in vain.
- **Listen intently:** Pay close attention to what decision makers share. Show them that their thoughts and feedback are truly valued.
- **Connect through shared challenges:** Show that you grasp the difficulties and pain points they are up against. A little empathy goes a long way. If your account team already has a strong working relationship with stakeholders, you may also wish to attempt to leverage the client by showcasing your messaging and some content items to ensure that your messaging is on point.
- **Be clear and straightforward:** Always be open and honest in your interactions. Provide clear, easy-to-understand details about what you offer. This should be true with your account team as well as the client. Do not try and promise outcomes upfront, instead show that you are there to listen and learn. As you create messaging and become included in discussions, the value added will be felt and seen.

Underpinning all these methods is the necessity of consistent communication. Showing up regularly is key to building trust and understanding. Regular engagement helps you stay connected with decision makers and keeps your business visible. Whether it's through scheduled conversations, e-mails, or calls, keeping a steady flow of communication builds familiarity and strengthens the ties you're building. I like to keep open lines of communication on multiple platforms with my teams.

This works not only when developing relationships with your target audience but also with the account team. All of these things that I've mentioned above can be reflected when building relationships with members of the account team. Because the perceived value you create with the account team is just as important as the real value you bring to the account.

The Tangible ROI of Hyperpersonalization

Hyperpersonalization tends to get tossed around a lot these days. And it really is just another piece of jargon marketers invented—something abstract and hard to put into words. But if you step back for a moment and think about the times someone genuinely understood what you needed before you even fully articulated it or offered a solution that felt made just for you. There's a distinct feeling to that interaction, isn't there? That feeling translates directly into business outcomes. It is almost like a feeling that you are communicating with someone without even speaking. To me, this is the ethos in the rhetorical triangle. Ethos relates to the credibility or trustworthiness of the person presenting or speaking, essentially their street cred.

Hyperpersonalization is about focusing sharply on individual customers, understanding their unique circumstances, and shaping every interaction around those specific needs. When done right, this approach moves beyond abstract concepts and delivers real, measurable impact. It's about driving revenue and building the kind of customer connections that last. Recently, I was working on an account where the Chief Information Officer (CIO), Dan, left his role for a major transportation and defense company. And we had created such a strong relationship, that he brought us in to pitch for him in his new CIO role. That's the power or Strategic ABM relationships.

Here are a few examples of how this focused type of effort works:

a. Boosting Your Odds and Growing the Pot
   Let's consider sales engagements. When an account team invests time to truly grasp a client's pain points, their goals, and the specific challenges they face, the conversation changes. It stops being

a generic pitch and becomes a discussion about tailored solutions. Strategic ABMers help convey that level of understanding, reflected in personalized outreach, playing a significant difference in developing targeted opportunities. Simply, it increases the likelihood of winning. What's more, by providing solutions that fit precisely, you aren't just winning; you're winning bigger deals. Addressing specific needs and opportunities directly increases the value delivered to the client and, consequently, the revenue from that single account. And if you're willing to take the risk then the rewards are impressive. Year over year I've seen significant growth with Strategic ABM accounts that have been in the program for more than 13 months. In one case we saw a growth of 40 percent of one account, due in part to the Strategic ABM efforts.

b. Tailoring Solutions for Growth

When you tailor your approach to a specific account's needs, you're not only increasing initial impact—you're naturally creating opportunities for upselling, cross-selling, and ongoing value creation. Done right, these conversations never feel like a push. They feel like progress.

A clear example of this comes from my work alongside Kyle McGrotty, a senior client manager. We were focused on securing a face-to-face meeting with a senior vice president (SVP) at a large, bicontinental health care provider. To support this, we launched a coordinated campaign: a highly targeted e-mail nurture paired with a LinkedIn outreach strategy, each customized around the client's known priorities.

As we monitored engagement through our marketing automation platform, we noticed that the SVP was consistently opening and clicking on links in our e-mails. This behavioral signal provided Kyle with the perfect window to follow-up personally referencing specific topics the SVP had shown interest in. We even crafted additional e-mails with links to other insights that Kyle could reference. That insight made the outreach not just timely but relevant. He said, "Sloan helped us open new doors which enabled us to educate our clients about new ways in which we could address their business needs. He understands the nuances of sales and account management very well, and he does all this with humility and proven experience." This is the type of peer respect and relationship you can expect from proper Strategic ABM execution.

Again, it's not just aligning with the target account; it's aligning with your account team as well. When you take the time, you will find yourself delivering insight that resonates, and success that doesn't feel forced. It feels earned.

c. Cutting Through the Noise

Hyperpersonalization doesn't just improve engagement—it speeds up the entire business process. When a message speaks directly to a decision maker's priorities, it stands out immediately. The typical time of back-and-forth to close/won shrinks. Conversations progress more quickly. And the likelihood of reaching a yes increases. **In short, relevance accelerates results.**

One of the key metrics I monitor within our CRM is **Opportunity Time to Close**. It's notoriously difficult to influence in many industries, especially when your sales cycle is well established. But I've always been fascinated by how to make the most of the time we have—and how we can unlock efficiency not just in marketing but across the full go-to-market team.

That's why embedding yourself with your account team is critical. Understanding their process, their roadblocks, and their day-to-day operations often reveals hidden opportunities for acceleration.

Years ago, I worked with a Seattle based home improvement company, Fox Plumbing & Heating, where the technicians—service specialists—were manually writing every estimate, invoice, and work order. At first glance, it seemed like a standard workflow. But in shadowing them, I realized this process was costing them an extra job per day. Not due to lack of demand, but inefficiency.

I brought this issue up with the owner, David Brown, and proposed a change: Move the team to a fully digital, end-to-end workflow. We implemented mobile solutions that allowed techs to generate estimates, verify parts and costs, and take payments—all on-site, in real time.

The result? Technicians added an average of one more job to their calendar per day. Customer satisfaction and retention rose.

Annual technician income increased by up to 20 percent. And within the first year, the business added over $8 million in profit in the first year.

This is the power of operational empathy and strategic problem-solving. In ABM, the same principle applies; when we create personal relevance not just the message but how we work with sales and delivery teams, we unlock capacity. We cut through complexity. And we drive faster, more meaningful outcomes—for everyone involved.

In 2013, the company that I managed and later owned was completely paper invoices. When we hired a Marketing Manager (Sloan Newman), we decided to go digital for invoices and pricing for customers to see for themselves. It was revolutionary for our business. That move greatly helped double our revenue in a three to four-year span. There are just so many roads to help grow your business and give the customers the best possible service. This is the best thing we could have done for Fox. —Chad Lindley, General Manager and Former Owner of Fox Plumbing and Heating

d. Building Lasting Bonds
Thinking about the long game, personal relevance always wins when you're building strong and enduring relationships. When customers sense they are understood and valued beyond a transaction, they are more likely to stick around. This means higher customer retention, less churn, and extended engagements that build customer lifetime value (CLV). These loyal customers don't just stay; they often become genuine advocates for your brand.

That is why I will only recommend existing accounts should be considered for 1:1 ABM campaigns. Swinging for the fence opportunities on new accounts can be put into Deal Acceleration, for when you aren't sure if you'll win the new logo or even if the account will still be around in 14 months.

I always follow the 80/20 rule during account selection. Because I spend a significant amount of investment and time working on these accounts, and I want to be sure that they are accounts that are planning to be around for the foreseeable future.

Bev Burgess, Dorothea Gosling, and the Inflexion Group teach and write about **Deal Acceleration.**[7] This process tends to be a type of streamlined version of Strategic ABM. It creates a way to bring ABM insights to large deal opportunities but without the level of depth that I am discussing here. Personally, I like to use Deal Acceleration for existing accounts with large opportunities with the hope that they transition into full Strategic ABM accounts. This is a good way to create your own growth account opportunities.

e. Standing Apart

In a crowded marketplace, differentiation is everything. Knowing your customers individually and being able to provide solutions that speak directly to their unique situations gives you a distinct advantage. It's how you distinguish yourself from the competition. This isn't just about a short-term gain; it provides a solid basis for sustained growth and long-term success.

Focusing on the individual customer isn't merely a strategy; it's a fundamental shift in how businesses connect and create value, with clear results on the bottom line.

Moving Beyond Generic Messaging in High-Value Deals

When you're talking to a key stakeholder, sending the same message you send to everyone else is like showing up to a formal dinner in flip-flops. It just doesn't fit. In the world of focusing intensely on specific, high-value client accounts, a message meant for the masses rarely turn heads. It skips over the details that matter to your target audience. To connect effectively, you need a different approach. It means knowing and speaking to what really matters to your audience of one.

By looking closely at their business environment, recent shifts in leadership, or major strategic moves, you can find places where what you offer provides something they genuinely need or addresses new directions

[7]Burgess (2017).

they're heading in. This kind of insight lets you frame your message in a way that might offer a fresh perspective or a new way to challenge them to think differently.

Crafting a message like this signals that you not only grasp the client's difficulties but are also serious about helping to fix them.

- Figure out your aligned goals.
- Spot the space where your value proposition fits their unmet needs.
- Think about how you're going to connect with the key stakeholders. Create a list of potential executive sponsors.
- Understand the challenges of the account team—do they struggle to reach certain people, deal with outdated systems, navigate a constantly changing group of buyers, or see clients not fully using what they bought? Ask questions.

Setting up just three primary pillars for your messaging means everything you do and say afterward can circle back to these main points, keeping things consistent and relevant.

To move past general statements, you must show concrete, tailored solutions that clearly explain the direct good things that will happen for that target account. This shows you understand their unique spot and are prepared to invest in solving their issues. By focusing on the value the account team can deliver, you build a meaningful link between the key stakeholders and the organization.

For success in working with target accounts, consider some practical steps:

- Create special opportunities that show you truly understand your audience, always thinking "white-glove" treatment.
- Make sure the message and the offerings you present are genuinely the best fit for the target account.
- Ensure everyone on your side—marketing, sales, and delivery—is communicating on how they talk about your position and value.

Executing on these methods will help your messaging to have a better chance of catching the attention of your target accounts. When you take a more focused approach in how you communicate, your entire organization will stand out from others and build a solid base for significant connections with the accounts that matter most. The result of all of this, is a method for working with target accounts that brings real outcomes, instead of just using broad messages that don't connect. Focusing on specific messages and careful research helps businesses realize the full potential of working with your team to achieve their aims.

Target Account Expectations in Today's World

Think about how you buy things today compared to even a few years ago. Five years ago, I leased a car where you had to plug in your phone for Apple CarPlay. However, today I can just start my car and the phone automatically connects. Technology is constantly changing our lives faster than any other point in history. And clients are no longer just looking for a product, platform, or service; they want experiences that feel like they were made just for them. They want interactions that recognize who they are, what they like, and what they need, right when they need it. This desire for something personal, relevant, and genuinely valuable is reshaping everyone's marketplace.

A big part of this change comes from how much time we all spend interacting digitally. Every app we use, every website we visit, every social media scroll sets a standard. These interactions teach us what good feels like, and they raise the bar for every company we deal with, whether it's online or in person. If a business wants to thrive now, it needs to truly get what makes each customer tick, focus on building real connections, and handle information with openness and integrity. Your job, across marketing, is to make sure you are regularly monitoring these changes. During COVID, I monitored how traffic was viewing our content. It was a 60:40 split of desktop to mobile. Post-COVID, that number has flipped. That means that the content we now create, I need to think of how it is loading and being seen on mobile first. This is just a simple example but an important one.

Creating a Personalized Experience

Personalization isn't optional anymore; it's essential for doing business. People anticipate interactions that are precisely shaped to their individual tastes and requirements. Making this happen involves using information and analysis to craft marketing efforts that hit the mark, suggest products people might need, and make everything online feel effortless. Look at what customers are expecting these days: service that anticipates needs, thought leadership from your C-suite on numerous topics, being a leader not only technically but also socially, conversations that feel personal, and experiences that flow smoothly across all the different places they interact with a company digitally.

Digital interactions are powerful sculptors of how people view a company. When engaging online feels easy and intuitive, it builds a positive impression. When it's difficult or frustrating, it does the opposite. Companies must prioritize adapting to the digital age, investing in the tools that enable personalized and linked experiences everywhere a customer might touch the brand.

What Matters Most to the Customer

In today's business landscape, the definition of value belongs squarely to the customer. It's no longer determined by what we think is valuable—it's shaped by what the customer perceives as meaningful and relevant. As representatives of our organizations, it's our job to truly understand what matters to them—and adjust our strategies accordingly.

That means going beyond surface-level personas or generic value propositions. It requires listening deeply, understanding their pain points, recognizing their priorities, and adapting to how they actually make decisions. Strategic ABM demands that we put the customer at the center of every conversation and every campaign.

When we do this well, something powerful happens we shift from selling solutions to co-creating success. The result is not only increased loyalty but, often, natural pathways to expansion—because the customer feels seen, supported, and understood.

Over the years, I've watched marketers enter the world of Strategic ABM and undergo a mindset transformation. At first, many approach it from a campaign perspective—focused on tactics and metrics. But as they work more closely with clients and account teams, they begin to shift. I've heard them say things like: "We need to do what's best for the client ...

even if that's not what's best for us right now" (Evan Jordan, Director of ABM and Client Engagement, NTT DATA).

That kind of thinking is at the heart of lasting growth. It's a reflection of true client empathy—and it's what separates transactional vendors from long-term partners.

Building Real Bonds

Making connections is incredibly important in the market today. Customers are seeking authentic bonds, not just quick transactions. Companies must make it a priority to build confidence and understanding with the people they serve, nurturing enduring relationships that encourage repeat business and enthusiastic recommendations. This comes from being open and principled in how customer data is handled, communicating in a way that feels personal, and committing to providing real benefit.

Confidentiality and earning confidence regarding data are vital parts of any successful customer relationship. Companies must emphasize transparency and ethics in their data practices, ensuring customer information is protected and used responsibly. By doing this, businesses can build confidence with the people they serve, driving both loyalty and business expansion.

The direction of customer experience is marked by swiftly changing expectations, the growing impact of digital interactions, and an increasing call for personalization and genuine connection. Companies that place the customer first, act with transparency, and operate ethically will be best positioned for success in this new era. By understanding what makes each customer unique and adjusting how they interact, businesses can build lasting connections that propel growth and loyalty.

Defining the 1:1 Approach

Engaging strategically with your 1:1 ABM selected accounts requires more than just targeted outreach—it demands precision, alignment, and a deep understanding of the people behind the business. The 1:1 ABM approach is built on tailored, insight-led interactions that deliver meaningful value across multiple layers of the account.

At the heart of it, this approach is about developing unique experiences for each account—rooted in relevance, empathy, and business impact. Success isn't measured by campaign-level key performance indicators (KPIs) alone, but by how your efforts move the needle on the account's actual goals, challenges, and aspirations.

And you should also know what you don't need to waste time reporting on:

- **Vanity metrics** (likes, impressions) unless directly tied to engagement
- **MQL volume**—this model isn't about leads
- **Attribution wars**—focus on **collaborative value**, not credit
- **Activities for their own sake** (e-mails sent ≠ progress)

If a metric doesn't help you decide what to do next, it's noise.

And alignment with the account team is critical. You must establish trust internally first making it clear that marketing is there not just to broadcast but to listen, support, and cocreate. As highlighted by Philip Kotler, Neil Rackham, and Suj Krishnaswamy in the *Harvard Business Review*, long-standing divides between sales and marketing can derail even the most thoughtful ABM efforts. Bridging that gap is the first step to building a unified front. To achieve this, we go through what we call an Onboarding process for the account team.[8]

The purpose of Onboarding an account is to make them aware of the tasks of marketing and educate them on the ABM process. We want them to know that this won't be a one-off campaign that they will be working with, that this is long-term investment in their account. That you are coming in as an additional member of the team to develop and strategize on how marketing can help to grow the portfolio with a specific account.

Once Onboarding is achieved, everything else builds on that foundation:

- **Account intelligence** becomes the lens through which personalization happens. If you have tools, vendors or specialists, then

[8]Philip Kotler (2006).

reach out to them as you begin the Onboarding process. Never wait on this step in the process.

- **Value creation** becomes the goal of every interaction—not just conversion.
- **Trust and relevance** become your most important metrics.

Consistent, meaningful engagement across the account team—combined with insights that demonstrate you understand their world—forms the basis of an approach that doesn't just win deals but strengthens relationships over time.

I created a questionnaire that I found to be helpful to present to the account team following the Onboarding process that allowed for initial feedback and showcased active listening from the ABM team. Shown in Figure 3.1 is a sample of the questionnaire created. It allowed for feedback as well as for qualitative data. We only associated it to the account so the responses would be able to remain anonymous. This idea was adapted from Philip Kotler, Neil Rackham, and Suj Krishnaswamy's research.

When 1:1 ABM is done right, it becomes less about "marketing to" an account and more about embedding yourself with the account team, gaining their respect and growing hand-in-hand with the account.

Tailoring the Journey

When you're trying to make a real connection in the business world, sending the same message to everyone just doesn't cut it. It's like trying to convince a chef they need more hammers when what they desperately need are sharper knives. ABM, especially the 1:1 ABM, asks us to throw out the mass mailer mindset and get personal. Really personal. We're talking about focusing intently on a single company, and really, just a handful of key stakeholders inside that company. This attention to detail means everything you say and do feels like it was made just for them.

Once you've aligned the account then you should have an audit of the account, a market insight drill. It makes sure that what you are hearing and seeing, is what the account team is hearing and seeing. This involves

Onboarding ABM Onboarding & Process Improvement Questionnaire

Your Role & Context

1. What account are you on?
Answer:

2. How long have you been engaged in the ABM program?
Less than 3 months 3-6 months 6-12 months. 12+ months

The Onboarding Experience

1. The ABM Onboarding process prepared me to participate effectively in the program.
(Strongly Agree, Agree, Neutral, Disagree, Strongly Disagree)
2. The ABM Onboarding content was relevant to my role and account responsibilities.
(Strongly Agree, Agree, Neutral, Disagree, Strongly Disagree)
3. The ABM Onboarding timeline and pacing were appropriate.
(Strongly Agree, Agree, Neutral, Disagree, Strongly Disagree)
4. ABM has taken an active stance with our team (creating value, regular feedback, development of relevant collateral, etc.).
(Strongly Agree, Agree, Neutral, Disagree, Strongly Disagree)
5. I can see and understand the value the ABM can bring to our team.
(Strongly Agree, Agree, Neutral, Disagree, Strongly Disagree)
6. What part of the onboarding process was most helpful?
Answer:
7. What part of the onboarding process could be improved or simplified?
Answer:

ABM Process Clarity

1. I understand the end-to-end ABM process (planning - activation - measurement).
(Strongly Agree, Agree, Neutral, Disagree, Strongly Disagree)
2. My responsibilities within the ABM process are clearly defined.
(Strongly Agree, Agree, Neutral, Disagree, Strongly Disagree)
3. Where do you experience the most friction or confusion in the ABM process?
Answer:

4. What steps in the ABM process feel unnecessary, redundant, or unclear?
Answer:

Tools, Resources & Workflow

1. The ABM tools and platforms support efficient execution of my work.
(Strongly Agree, Agree, Neutral, Disagree, Strongly Disagree)
2. Templates, playbooks, and guides are easy to find and use.
(Strongly Agree, Agree, Neutral, Disagree, Strongly Disagree)
3. Are there any tools, platforms or resources slowing you down in connecting with your account?
Answer:

4. What tools, templates, or automation would improve the ABM workflow?
Answer:

Execution & Application

1. I feel confident with the direction of the Strategic 1:1 ABM strategy to his/her leadership.
(Strongly Agree, Agree, Neutral, Disagree, Strongly Disagree)
2. The ABM process appears to integrate well with how I already work day to day. responsibilities.
(Strongly Agree, Agree, Neutral, Disagree, Strongly Disagree)
3. The members of the ABM team are solution-oriented to issues regarding reputation and relationships.
(Strongly Agree, Agree, Neutral, Disagree, Strongly Disagree)
4. ABM is providing opportunities to develop new opportunities for engagements and conversations with the account.
(Strongly Agree, Agree, Neutral, Disagree, Strongly Disagree)
5. Describe a moment where ABM processes either helped or hindered account execution.
Answer:

Collaboration & Alignment

1. Collaboration between Sales, Account and ABM team has been effective..
(Strongly Agree, Agree, Neutral, Disagree, Strongly Disagree)
2. Decision-making from the ABM process is clear and timely.
(Strongly Agree, Agree, Neutral, Disagree, Strongly Disagree)
3. What process changes would improve cross-function collaboration?
Answer:

Process Improvement & Optimization

1. What is the single biggest process improvement that would make ABM more effective for you?
Answer:

2. Which ABM process should be prioritized for improvement next?
a. Account planning
b. Campaign activation
c. Measurement & reporting
d. Tools & data
e. Governance & approvals
f. Communication & alignment

3. How often should ABM processes be reviewed and optimized?
g. Quarterly
h. Bi-annually
i. Annually
j. As needed

4. Any additional feedback or suggestions to improve the ABM onboarding or ongoing processes?
Answer:

Figure 3.1 Sales ABM questionnaire

digging into how they operate day-to-day, what's happening in their industry, and the specific problems they face. And you need to spend at least an hour with the account team reviewing these insights. This is where the agility in Strategic ABM comes into play. You need to either be able to pull this report together, or if you're lucky have a Market Insights team of analysts that can ensure an unbiased review.

This audit will help you to understand how decisions get made inside that company. Who are the main players? Who and what influences them? What roles do different people have in deciding what to buy? Knowing this network helps you craft messages and materials that speak directly to each person, making it much more likely they'll see the value. It also gives the account team the chance to discuss any roadblocks or issues they currently have with these key individuals.

A vital part of Strategic ABM is mapping out the path an account takes, from first hearing about you to becoming a strong supporter. This path has distinct steps. First, there's **Awareness**, making the account aware that they might have a problem and a solution exists. Then comes **Consideration**, where they look at different options, weighing things like cost and how it might work for them. After that, the **Decision** is made. Next is **Implementation**, getting the chosen solution up and running. Finally, you get the win with **Advocacy**. Happy key stakeholders start talking positively about you, perhaps providing testimonials, and sending others in their company your way. Pinpointing the key interactions at each step—e-mails, calls, content they look at, meetings, thought leadership, invitations to once-in-a-lifetime events—helps make sure each experience feels personal.

Content is essential in this kind of marketing. It's how you deliver those personal messages along the account's path. The materials should offer useful insights, solutions, and stories that fit the account's specific situation and challenges. This could mean providing:

- Reports about their industry, pointing out trends and challenges relevant to their work.
- Case Studies showing how companies like theirs have seen success with your solution.
- White Papers that offer deep analysis and ways to tackle specific problems they face.

Making communication personal also means thinking about how the account prefers to communicate. Do they like e-mail, phone calls, social media, or meeting face-to-face? Respecting these preferences means your outreach feels welcomed and valued, not like an interruption.

Making a Strategic ABM strategy work for the long haul means always looking for ways to do it better based on what the account and the account team tells you, directly as well as indirectly. Checking often how different interactions are landing and being agile enough to adjust keeps your approach sharp and effective. This involves:

- Asking for input regularly.
- Checking how the target account interacts with different materials and messages to understand what works. A/B testing of messages and creating "this, then that" e-mail nurture strategies to help prep the audience.
- Changing what you say and how you say it based on this feedback and interaction data. Never use the same tone of voice for every account. Be aware of their culture and how they speak.
- Challenging how your target account thinks. You need to have something to say that makes people notice you and listen. Sometimes that means challenging how a target account has been doing business and suggesting a new path forward.

By focusing this way and constantly refining things, you can build a truly specific and effective 1:1 ABM strategy that connects with the companies you care about and leads to meaningful results.

Focus on Needs and Goals

Stepping into the arena of target account engagement demands a shift in perspective. It's not about shouting your message into the void hoping someone listens; it's about having a focused conversation with the select few who truly matter. When you zero in on Strategic ABM, that conversation requires something more: It requires knowing the other person, or rather, the account, inside and out, and knowing what makes you different from your competitors.

Data is the foundation to being able to accomplish this goal. Think of it as gathering the intel you need to understand precisely what makes a specific account tick, what they're trying to achieve, and what fears live in their closets. This kind of detailed understanding allows ABM to craft messages and approaches built specifically for that one account's distinct situation and aspirations.

Strategic ABM centers on truly grasping the specific requirements of each account and building marketing strategies directly from that understanding. This way of working acknowledges that no two accounts are alike. Each has its own set of hurdles, objectives, and ways they make decisions. By gaining this detailed view of these elements, ABMers can put together bespoke plans that speak directly to what the account needs.

The understanding gained from this deep research directly informs the creation of tailored strategies and custom solutions. This process involves working with the account to build value propositions that connect with their highest priorities and their toughest challenges. It makes certain that whatever you communicate is relevant, well-timed, and has real impact. Take, for example, one situation where a targeted ABM effort revealed a surprising issue: a client's firewall was blocking standard HTML e-mails. This meant less than 1 percent of messages were even opened. I worked with our marketing automation team to create an A/B test where we would send out versions of a traditional marketing HTML e-mail and then one coming from the CE that was plain text and personalized. The open rates for C-suite executives jumped by 44 percent. Click-through rates soared past 70 percent, far exceeding typical results for the industry.

Ensuring marketing efforts line up with account aims is critically important in Strategic ABM. This ensures that marketing isn't just made for each account's needs, but also directly helps them succeed. By clearly showing you understand their objectives and are committed to helping them reach them, marketers can build confidence and establish strong, cooperative working relationships alongside the account team. At one point we had to pause a campaign for three months due to an RFP. We were concerned that our 1:1 ABM efforts would disqualify us from the bid process. I was able to quickly execute the pause due to the regular communications and open dialogue with the account team.

To show effectively how your marketing work will help an account succeed, focus on creating and sharing valuable, useful content. This content should aim to address particular problems with practical solutions that fit with the account's needs. This allows you to position yourself as a trusted advisor and partner who helps solve problems for the account team.

Designing High-Touch Interaction Frameworks

Getting anywhere meaningful in business often comes down to understanding people. It's not just about having a great product or service; it's about knowing who holds the cards, who influences the game, and what their poker face looks like. Think about zeroing in on specific, target accounts. To make real headway there, grasping who the important figures are isn't just helpful, it's necessary for a successful Strategic ABM program. Knowing these individuals lets you shape what you say and do in ways that land with impact, building stronger connections and getting things done with those you care about most.

The very first step in this focused approach is figuring out who matters inside that target account. These aren't just random names; they are the individuals who either sign-off on purchases or significantly sway the people who do. Picture the senior leadership, like the CEO or chief financial officer (CFO), maybe department heads wrestling with specific challenges, or other senior managers whose opinions carry weight. Identifying these key stakeholders is your bedrock. In Strategic ABM, this is your primary audience.

Once you've got their names then it is time to go to work. You'll need to map out their roles and what they're responsible for. Sales Navigator from LinkedIn has an amazing tool that allows for you to accomplish and share it with your account team via your CRM. This means digging a bit to understand their daily grind, the problems they face, and what they're ultimately trying to achieve. When you know this stuff, you can start crafting messages and experiences that feel truly relevant to each person. It's like speaking their language, making every interaction more meaningful.

That brings us to personal relevance. You're going to need to make decisions about what custom-built experiences will have the greatest impact while reflecting what you know about that specific stakeholder's needs and interests. Again, this goes back to becoming the CMO of your target accounts.

Achieving this level of personalization requires looking beyond the obvious. You need to gather insights that give you a clearer picture of their preferences and how they behave. This might involve seeing how they interact with your website, looking at their activity on professional networks, or analyzing their digital footprints. It's about understanding your audience. If you nail this then the rest is easy-peasy.

You always need to be considering that your interactions need a human touch. High-touch interactions are vital for building solid connections and truly engaging those important accounts. These are the moments that feel personal—a well-timed e-mail that shows you understand their world, a phone call that offers genuine help, or even a face-to-face meeting or introduction to an analyst that can help them identify solutions.

Making sure these interactions work together is key. It's important to coordinate how you reach out across different channels so that the message is always consistent. Think of it like conducting an orchestra; every instrument plays its part, but they follow the same score. This prevents disjointed experiences and ensures that each stakeholder receives a clear, unified message, no matter how they interact.

Finally, success of Strategic 1:1 ABM depends on constantly building on what you've accomplished. Setting up feedback loops for continuous improvement is essential. Having regular audits of how accounts are responding to your efforts and adjusting your approach based on what you learn. This includes ongoing monitoring and tweaking your strategy to get the best possible results that lead to change.

The Difference Between Personalization and Customization in 1:1

Let's face it—U.S. marketers spent nearly $60 billion in 2015 on digital ads, but the industry doesn't do a great job connecting people with products they want.

—Sathvik Tantry, "Making Personalized Marketing Work," *Harvard Business Review*[9]

[9] Tantry (2016).

Stepping into the world of Strategic ABM, you quickly realize it's not just marketing anymore. It's not about reaching many; it's about truly connecting with a select few. As Tantry observed, personalized marketing holds great potential to increase engagement and conversion—but most companies fail to execute it effectively. Even with massive investments, personalization often stops at surface-level gestures instead of creating real, resonant connections. Success in 1:1 ABM isn't measured in clicks or impressions—it's measured in conversations, introductions, and the depth of trust built between teams.

And getting that connection right often brings up a question that trips up many teams: are we *personalizing* or are we *customizing*? Knowing the difference isn't just academic; it directly impacts your effort, spend, and whether you move the needle on revenue.

Think of it this way: personalization is like walking into a high-end store where the staff already knows your size and preferred styles from past visits. They bring out clothes from their existing collection that are likely to fit you perfectly and suit your taste. It's efficient, it feels tailored to you, but it's built on what they already have on the racks. This is personalization in 1:1 ABM. You use the information you have about an account—their industry challenges, who you've spoken to before, what content they've engaged with—to adapt your existing messages and content. You might change the opening of an e-mail to reference their specific business goal or show website content that highlights solutions relevant to their known issues. It's about adapting what exists to make it relevant. This approach lets you connect with several target accounts without reinventing the wheel each time.

Customization, on the other hand, is ordering a completely bespoke suit. You start from scratch, choosing the fabric, the cut, every single detail, built precisely for your unique measurements and preferences. This takes considerably more time, requires specialist skills, and costs more. Customization means creating something entirely new for a single account. Maybe they have a challenge so specific that none of your current case studies or standard product materials address it. You might build a unique solution proposal deck, develop a custom demonstration environment, or create entirely new content addressing their one-of-a-kind situation. It demands significant investment—in time, in the team working on it, and in budget.

The two approaches have distinct footprints when you look at them side-by-side. Scalability is a major one; you can personalize experiences for many accounts relatively easily because you're reusing and adapting. Customization is inherently 1:1 ABM; building something entirely new for multiple accounts simply isn't feasible for most teams. Naturally, the resource intensity follows personalization using data and smart systems to adapt, while customization requires dedicated human effort to build from zero. While both can grab attention, customization often has the potential for deeper, lasting impact because it's built precisely for that account's unique situation. And speaking of data, personalization relies heavily on having good information to know how to adapt content. Customization, while still needing data, places a greater premium on a truly deep, almost intuitive understanding of the account's specific business, their internal politics, and their exact needs.

Starting from zero can make people nervous when it comes to investment but that doesn't mean you can't find the sweet spot. You can. And when you do, you will be able to unlock real effectiveness in you 1:1 ABM campaigns and see a worthwhile return on your efforts. Use personalization where you can efficiently connect with your target accounts, making them feel heard and understood without needing a massive team. But you also need to know when an account warrants customization—typically those high-value accounts with complex, specific problems that only a unique solution will address. Always think about how customization can be scalable for a larger group of accounts.

Striking the right balance begins with an honest assessment of your internal capabilities. Take stock of your team's skills, your available budget, and the technologies at your disposal. Do you have the right data and platforms to enable true personalization? Do you have the time and expertise to develop custom content or experiences? Alongside this internal audit, it's equally important to deeply understand your target accounts. What are their priorities? What challenges are they facing? What are their desired outcomes?

This clarity helps you determine whether you can adapt existing content or need to build something entirely new. And just as importantly—it's not a one-and-done decision. ABM requires continuous observation, iteration, and refinement. You need to stay responsive, learning from what works (and what doesn't), and adjusting accordingly.

Mastering the balance between adaptation and creation isn't just a tactical decision—it's a strategic one. It's what elevates 1:1 ABM from simply being "customized marketing" to becoming a true engine of relationship growth. When you've spent 6 to 12 months embedded in a single account—when you've seen trust deepen, conversations evolve, and opportunities emerge—it's a powerful reminder of why this work matters. There's no greater reward than witnessing the real, lasting impact that leads to real change.

CHAPTER 4

Identifying and Selecting Your Strategic Accounts

You can't hit a target you cannot see, and you cannot see a target you do not have.

Zig Ziglar[10]

The Right Stuff: Proper Account Selection

Zig Ziglar's quote references that you need to know where your target was, where it is, and have a good understanding of where it's going. When pursuing major growth opportunities through Strategic ABM, focus is everything. Directing time and resources toward the wrong accounts—those that don't align with your goals or lack meaningful potential—can quickly drain momentum and yield minimal return. No matter how creative or ambitious your marketing plan is if it isn't driving revenue for the business. It's not delivering value.

That's why setting clear goals and validating account potential early is essential. Misalignment can lead to costly missteps. Imagine investing four months into a 1:1 ABM campaign, only to realize that the account you were told had $130 million in the pipeline when in reality it has $13 million—and the potential target account isn't publicly traded. Situations like this are avoidable with the right vetting process upfront.

ABM gives us a structured and strategic framework to avoid these pitfalls. Instead of trying to play a round of eighteen with only your driver, ABM channels effort into a select group of high-value accounts—those most likely to benefit from your solution and grow alongside your

---

[10]Ziglar (1977).

organization. ABM provides you with all the clubs in your bag. The foundation of this approach is building your **Ideal Strategic Account Profile (ISAP)** or **Ideal Client Profile (ICP)**. This isn't just a list of firmographics—it's a qualification framework that filters the noise and helps you identify accounts with real partnership potential (Figure 4.1).

When building an ISAP for ABM Framework, consider factors such as:

- Potential for long-term revenue and upsell opportunities
- Strategic alignment between your organizations
- Willingness to collaborate across multiple stakeholders
- Internal readiness to engage (infrastructure, bandwidth, culture)
- Existing relationship history with regards to the broader organization

In the early stages of building a Strategic ABM program, it's smart to go after the "low-hanging fruit"—accounts that already have healthy relationships or historical engagement with your brand. These accounts often respond more quickly to personalized outreach and provide stronger internal champions to codevelop initiatives.

One simple yet powerful indicator for B2B marketers with limited resources is whether a target account already has a Master Service Agreement (MSA) in place. An MSA typically signals that the account has been through legal review and holds a preestablished relationship with your organization—making onboarding smoother and reducing risk. Even better, review the MSA to check for marketing permissions or restrictions. If an account prohibits public case studies or logo usage, it may limit your ability to create impactful campaigns and thought leadership. While not always a deal-breaker, it's an important consideration.

Ultimately, strong account selection starts with strategic clarity. The accounts you choose to pursue will shape everything that follows—from messaging and campaign design to stakeholder engagement and ROI. Choose wisely, and you lay the groundwork for deeper relationships and greater impact.

Ideal Strategic Account Profile for ABM Framework

	Qualitative research and influential key stakeholder mapping	**Qualitative Analysis** Collect external data based for potential target accounts, such as annual reporting, google reports, IDC, or other third-party market insights	**Quantitative Analysis** Review internal data based on annual revenue from accounts, current pipeline opportunities, existing leadership relationships	**Predictive Analysis** Review forward-looking market data to understand where they are most likely to invest over the next 24 months
	Categorize insights into an ISAP mapping and potential strategic alignment	**Firmographics** Document company size, industry, location, annual revenue, and number of total employees	**Psychographics** Document the current attitude toward or reputation of your company by potential target account's key decision makers	**Signals/Technographics** Document what technologies your key stakeholders are engaged with—as key stakeholders become younger, the way to engage may be on nonconventional platforms
	ABM alignment and personalization	**Sales** Ensure the account team has an up-to-date account plan in place, there are strong existing relationships in place and can handle the additional asks of the ABM team	**Marketing** Ensure that the ABM team has the tools and content available to target and reach key audiences and ensure that only ABM messaging will be presented to key stakeholders	**Customer Success** CS should help ensure relationships continue to grow over time and provide insights into any unforeseen changes to be aware of how to adapt

Figure 4.1 Ideal strategic account profile for ABM framework

Defining the ISAP

Think for a moment about scattering seeds everywhere, hoping some might sprout. That approach might yield a few results, but it's hardly the most efficient way to grow a garden. Business often works similarly. Without a clear idea of where to plant your efforts, you risk wasting precious time and resources on ground that simply won't yield much of a harvest. This is where strategic focus becomes not just helpful but necessary.

ABM offers a different path. It's about identifying the specific soil that's most fertile and concentrating your energy there. And understanding the process to turn that soil, till it, and soften it to build those opportunities. At the heart of this focused strategy lies the ISAP. Defining your ISAP framework provides a way to see which potential accounts truly fit your long-term goals and offer the best possibilities for mutual growth. It's the process of picking the right ground before you even start planting. This focus ensures resources are used wisely, aimed directly at the accounts holding the greatest promise.

Key Components of the ISAP

Building this profile isn't just a single consideration; it involves looking at several distinct areas. The ISAP takes shape around factors like how much money an account might represent, how well they align with your own company's direction, and their willingness to work together.

- Revenue Potential
  Naturally, a central piece of the ISAP is understanding the money involved. This means looking at both the immediate financial gain and what the future might hold. Consider their current spending with you, how much they could potentially grow, and whether there are opportunities to sell them more or different things. Prioritizing accounts with significa1nt pipeline opportunities helps justify the financial investment for the focused attention and personal approach that Strategic ABM demands.
- Strategic Fit
  But it's not just about the finances. Assessing strategic fit means seeing if your core beliefs and where you both want to go in the long

run line up. When values are shared and there's a common picture of the future, the partnerships that develop tend to be stronger and last longer. This shared outlook makes successful work together much more likely. It also lets you shape your message and what you offer so it genuinely speaks to the account's particular requirements and aims.

- Organizational Readiness
  How ready the target account is to work together and try new things is another important test. You need to look at their general way of operating, how they make decisions, and if they seem open to adopting new ways of doing things or using new products. An account that is open to ABM methods is much more likely to participate effectively and find real value from working with you.

Developing an Effective ISAP

Creating a good ISAP requires collaboration. You need to work closely with the people who know the accounts best—the account teams. Together, you define shared goals and figure out what unique value you bring to these specific clients. This means doing some homework: understanding their market, noting any recent changes in leadership, or recognizing shifts in their own strategy. This research helps shape communication that suggests fresh ways of thinking about or engaging with them. Setting up three core pillars for your message ensures that everything you say or do going forward builds a clear and compelling story.

Benefits of a Well-Defined ISAP

Having a clearly defined ISAP brings distinct advantages.

- **Better account selection:** By choosing accounts based on their potential for revenue, strategic compatibility, and openness to partnership, businesses can direct their efforts toward the most promising chances.
- **Improved connection:** A focused ABM approach makes it possible to create specific messages and offerings that genuinely connect with an account's particular needs and aims.

- **Increased partnership worth:** By helping build stronger and more lasting working relationships, target accounts will drive long-term expansion and income.

By understanding the ISAP, you're able to establish a solid foundation for your ABM efforts, leading to more effective connections and, finally, more revenue growth.

Financial Indicators and Potential Lifetime Value

In marketing and sales, we spend a good amount of time discussing and identifying the "ideal customer profile," that perfect blend of characteristics that suggests a company might need what you offer. But what if I told you there's a deeper layer to peel back, something that tells you not just if they could use your solution but if they can invest in it and truly grow with it? It's the financial pulse of the target account, and in ABM, closely listening to that pulse is fundamental. In many ways ABM takes cues from the Social Penetration Theory (SPT), aka the Onion Model, developed by Altman and Taylor in 1987.[11] There are many layers for selecting the correct accounts when developing your ISAP.

Think about it. You might have the most tailored, insightful campaign ready for a target account, but if their finances are strained and they don't have money, that brilliant outreach might fall flat. Understanding an account's financial strength is important in directing personalized ABM efforts toward those most likely to engage, purchase, and expand. It signals their capacity to spend and their potential to partner for the long haul. This can also occur in certain industries when considering 1:Few or ABM Lite approaches.

One obvious place to start looking is their annual revenue. This isn't just a number; it's an indicator of their current scale and their presence in the market. Companies bringing in substantial revenue typically have more resources at their disposal. This often translates into larger budgets and, importantly, a greater need for sophisticated solutions that can help them manage that scale or push for further dominance. Targeting

[11]Taylor (1987).

accounts with significant revenue means focusing your energy where there's a higher probability of finding both the need and the willingness to invest.

A large company standing still or stagnating isn't always the best bet for a Strategic ABM account. *You may want to look at accounts where the growth rate shows more opportunity.* A company that's growing rapidly is a signal of future potential and, critically, evolving needs. As operations expand, new challenges arise, creating demand for solutions that can support that expansion. High-growth accounts are frequently more open to innovative solutions because they actively seek ways to fuel and manage their trajectory. Rapid growth often comes with increasing budgets, making them prime candidates for Strategic ABM.

We cannot forget the need for profitability. While revenue shows scale and growth shows momentum, profitability reveals sustainability. A company that consistently turns a healthy profit demonstrates financial stability. These are the businesses less likely to be held back by tight purse strings when a valuable solution comes along. Profitable accounts tend to be more confident in making investments aimed at improving efficiency or driving further success. Their ability to weather economic trade winds means they are more reliable long-term partners and will be great candidates as you evolve your ABM program of onboarding and offboarding.

Finally, connect these current indicators to the future with **lifetime value (LTV)**. LTV tends to be defined as the (Average Purchase Value × Purchase Frequency) × Average Customer Lifespan. Another way to find this is to take the Average Revenue Per User (ARPU) / the Churn Rate, where churn rate is the percentage of customers lost over a period. This metric looks at the total revenue you can expect from an account over your entire engagement. When accounts show strong revenue, growth, and profitability, they often correlate with a high-potential LTV. These are the accounts that justify significant, personalized 1:1 ABM investment. Focusing ABM efforts on high LTV accounts means concentrating resources where the ROI is likely to be greatest, ensuring that every tailored message and dedicated resource is applied to maximum effect.

These stated financial indicators—revenue, growth, profitability, and potential LTV—will provide a foundational understanding of whether a target account is more than just a 'good fit.' It will make your target account a viable, willing, and potentially high-value partner for ABM initiatives. These hidden signals will help to guide you to make smart targeting decisions.

Strategic Fit, Market Position, and Growth Potential

Finding the right ABM account isn't just about identifying a need—it's about recognizing a strategic fit. True alignment goes far beyond surface-level attributes like industry or company size. It's about shared values, complementary ways of working, and the potential to build a partnership that feels less like vendor-client and more like co-creators of progress.

To assess your fit, start by looking closely at how the target account operates within its market. Are they a dominant leader, a hungry challenger, or a specialized niche player? This context shapes everything—from the tone of your outreach to the type of value you bring to the table. A market leader may need help defending their position or scaling innovation. A challenger may be seeking fresh thinking that gives them an edge. Niche players often look for highly tailored expertise that resonates within their unique ecosystem.

Beyond where the account stands today, ask where they're headed. Do they have clear indicators of growth? Are there signs of investment, expansion, or organizational transformation? Strategic ABM is a resource-intensive approach, so it's critical to focus your energy where there's potential for meaningful return. Accounts with room to grow—whether it's through new offerings, market entry, or digital evolution—are often your best bets.

Understanding an account's long-term goals and strategic priorities also plays a part in this discussion. What are their biggest initiatives over the next 12 to 24 months? What problems are they trying to solve, and what outcomes matter most to them? When you build your messaging and engagement strategy around those drivers, you show the account that you've done your homework—and more importantly, that you're serious about helping them succeed. This kind of relevance is at the heart of *The Challenger Sale* by Matthew Dixon and Brent Adamson[12]: the best sales and marketing efforts don't just respond—they challenge and lead.

[12]Dixon (2011).

One experience that's stuck with me was a visit to Magdeburg, Germany in 2009, where I toured the Green Citadel of Magdeburg (*Grüne Zitadelle*). Designed by the bold and unconventional Friedensreich Hundertwasser, it's a building unlike any other—playful, vibrant, intentionally imperfect. To me, it symbolizes the kind of account I love working with, willing to push boundaries, think differently, and take bold steps forward. Strategic ABM is a journey, and the best partners are the ones willing to travel that road with curiosity, not caution.

Ultimately, identifying strategic fit means evaluating multiple dimensions at once:

- Cultural and operational alignment
- Technology compatibility
- Mutual understanding of success
- Market position and growth trajectory
- Willingness to innovate and collaborate

Yes, it can be daunting at first. But once you develop a rhythm—your process for analyzing, qualifying, and engaging accounts—you begin to see patterns more clearly. You stop guessing and start knowing which accounts will flourish with the kind of partnership that Strategic ABM will create.

Relationship Maturity and Accessibility

Creating a Strategic ABM program can feel like drawing up blueprints for a complex building. You design the structure, plan the systems, and figure out the materials. But what if the ground you're building on isn't solid?

The truth about successful 1:1 ABM campaigns aren't just in the strategy or that they are clever campaigns. It starts with something much more fundamental: the strength of your existing connections. How well do you really know the people inside the accounts you want to work with? Their willingness to talk, to listen, to see you as a partner—that makes all the difference. This isn't a minor detail; it's one of the first things I ask when onboarding accounts. You need to understand how deep those ties go, how easy it is to tap the right people, and use that understanding to pick the accounts where we can actually get things done.

Understanding Connections

To see if an ABM effort has a real chance, you have to gauge the quality of the connections you already have with the target account. Are they just contacts, or are they people who might speak up for your solutions? Will they give you honest feedback about what's happening inside their company? A strong connection is worth its weight in gold when building your initial messaging and content and having someone who can act as a focus group for your efforts.

When you look at existing connections, think about:

- People who can champion your ideas: Find those individuals who might informally back what you offer and tell you how your message lands.
- Mapping your contacts: Draw out who the key people are, what they do, what matters to them, and how much sway they have within their company.
- Past conversations: Look back at how you've talked to and worked with these main contacts before. What does that tell you about how solid the connection is?

You might think that doing this with accounts is cheating. Nothing is further from the truth. Strategic ABM is not meant to be a cold call engagement. The best Strategic ABM accounts are those that have solid relationships with key stakeholders that have large opportunities for growth. Just because one VP is an advocate for your company doesn't mean that his colleague knows you from Adam.

Finding the Way In

Even with several advocates, you will still need to work to find a way to create personal relevance with other key stakeholders.

Consider these points:

- **Company structure:** Figure out the company's setup. Who holds the power? Are there people who control access or those who can influence the outcome?
- **Ways to talk:** Pinpoint the best methods to get your message to the important individuals.

Internal Readiness and Resource Availability

Embarking on a 1:1 ABM journey isn't something you casually dive into. It demands a hard, honest look inward before anything outward takes shape. Before you target that dream account, before the first e-mail or event is planned, you have to ask: **Are we truly ready for this?**

Success in Strategic ABM begins with internal alignment. It requires the right mindset, the right champions, and the right resources to deliver a level of personalization that's meaningful and scalable. Simply put: if your internal house isn't in order, it doesn't matter how attractive your target list is—your strategy won't stick.

I've found success in this space not because I'm the best marketer in the room, but because I know ABM is a team sport. I look for people smarter than me: people who aren't afraid to say, "We've never done this before … but we're willing to try."

One of the first times I heard that was early in my career, fresh out of graduate school, when I suddenly became the entire Business Development team at MS&L London. My manager had departed the company, and I was thrown into the deep end. I found myself reporting directly to the CEO, Stuart Wilson. He gave me many life lessons and insights that I carry with me to this day. He taught me, "of all the things you can screw up, never get the client's name wrong." And more importantly he taught me to never be afraid to go big when you want to get creative.

In 2008, we caught wind that Virgin was shortlisting agencies for their new Public Relations Agency of Record (AOR). We weren't on the list, but Stuart desperately wanted to be considered for this opportunity. We needed to be bold. Virgin, led by Sir Richard Branson, was known for outrageous ideas. As a longtime fan, I knew we had to do something impressive.

At that time, Krispy Kreme had recently launched in London. As a proud South Carolinian, I was well aware of their legendary appeal. So, I bought two dozen donuts. One box remained untouched. The second? Our team rebranded it. We designed a custom MS&L London sleeve and inserted a laminated page styled like Virgin's website—but renamed it: *Why MS&L London*. And the outside of the box was designed to look like MS&L with a logo and colors. And then we made sure that we had all fresh donuts in each box. Finally, we carefully couriered the package and had it delivered directly to Virgin's head of PR department.

We started this mad concept on Wednesday. By Friday at 2:00 p.m., our idea was in the hands of Virgin. By 4:00 p.m., Stuart Wilson—whose name was printed on that personalized insert—received a call from Virgin to set up a meeting.

That moment stayed with me, not just because it worked but because it proved a fundamental truth: **When you rally a smart team around a bold idea, with urgency and intent, powerful things happen.**

Leadership Buy-In and Executive Sponsorship

Once you've decide to commit to Strategic ABM, securing **executive alignment** is nonnegotiable. Leadership support isn't symbolic—it's strategic. You need senior champions to serve as **Executive Sponsors**. These individuals don't just lend credibility; they open doors.

A committed sponsor can make introductions, connect dots within complex org charts, and engage peer-to-peer with key stakeholders in a way that marketing or sales alone can't. They signal seriousness. They cut through noise. And they help align internal and external stakeholders around mutual value.

Practical Methods for Identification

I want to move from an overview of account selection to a more practical step-by-step process. Moving from broad market outreach to concentrated efforts on specific businesses requires a deliberate process. Deciding which accounts warrant this special attention is foundational to success. This process begins by examining the knowledge already held within your organization—the history, interactions, and potential hidden in your records. Gaining clarity from these internal sources is the essential first step. The process then builds upon this foundation, extending to understanding the wider market context, defining clear standards for selection, and ensuring everyone involved agrees on the direction.

Leveraging Internal Data (CRM, Intent, Sales Insights, Service Records)

Choosing which target accounts for Strategic ABM isn't blind guesswork. It's using the information you already have inside your own walls. Internal information gives you a clear view of who you already work with and where the biggest chance for future opportunities lie. Looking closely at things like your customer records, what your sales team knows, and customer feedback from your service calls can help you truly understand the businesses that are most important to you. This understanding lets you make choices based on facts, and when you are starting to build your initial Strategic ABM program, you need to start with the facts.

Review your account records. These tell you so much about the opportunities in the pipeline, the size of deals, and how long you've known certain key businesses. By examining this data, you can spot accounts that show signs of making a lot of money for you, those you're already working with, and those you already have good relationships with. This will also help you to develop your True North of what qualifies as a potential Strategic ABM account.

Next, what does the account team see in their daily lives working on the account. Their notes and observations offer insight into what's happening in the market, where there are chances to grow, and how different business types are doing. When you look at sales information, you get a better sense of how the market moves and where you might be able to get bigger. For example, I tend to only consider accounts that have an account plan in place, and that it has been updated in the last four months. This helps in quickly dismissing potential Strategic ABM accounts that just aren't mature enough for the program. And it provides goal posts for accounts to strive for that want to be considered for the program.

Then there is customer feedback. This offers a different view of how happy your customers are, what problems they face, and what troubles them. Reading through service notes provides insight into whether accounts are happy, with a strong past of working well together and being satisfied. These are businesses where you might find ways to do more business with them. On the flip side, customer feedback provides insight into accounts that are having trouble. You can decide to bring in a target account with emerging issues to help keep concerns from growing into larger issues.

To figure out which target accounts are the most important to concentrate on, you should look for some specifics:

- Signs of bringing on several pipeline opportunities over the next 6 to 12 months.
- Have a history of a positive attitude working with you and have records of good relations.
- Culturally, they fit with where you are and where you want to go.

By focusing on target accounts that meet these points, makes the development of your Strategic and other ABM programs much smoother and likely to be adopted quicker.

To make the best use of the information you have inside your company, try these steps:

- Bring your information sources together. Combine customer records, sales observations, and service notes to get a full picture of your most important businesses. Consider dashboards in your CRM or using tools like Power Bi to be able to see everything on one screen. Power Bi is a popular business analytics tool from Microsoft, it allows users to connect to and visualize data from multiple sources. It creates interactive reports and dashboards and allows you to easily share insights across an organization.
- Look at your information often. Checking the data regularly means you stay aware of how your accounts are changing and what's happening in the market.

- Let your information guide your choices. Use the data to help you pick your first round of targets. Don't be swayed by personal desires from leadership.

Market Research and Industry Analysis

ABM flips the script on traditional marketing. Instead of broadcasting to broad segments, you're narrowing your focus to a handful of high-value accounts. To do this effectively, you need a deep understanding of the landscape your target accounts operate in.

Strong market research helps you answer key questions before you ever launch a campaign:

- Who should we target?
- What do they care about?
- Where is their company heading?

Understanding the forces shaping your target industry—emerging trends, challenges, and innovations—gives you clarity on which accounts are worth pursuing. That starts with gathering insights from industry reports, analyst publications, and customer conversations. For instance, a report on increased cloud adoption signals a cluster of accounts that may soon require modernization services. These trends guide not only who you target, but also how you speak to their evolving needs.

Feedback from industry insiders and end users adds another critical layer. The best account selection strategies start with empathy: what are people in this space frustrated by? What problems haven't been solved yet? That's where you can step in with relevance and differentiation.

Competitive analysis is just as essential. What are your competitors doing well? Where are they falling short? Understanding their positioning helps you spot gaps in the market—and highlight your unique strengths. One tool I often rely on for this is Klue, a competitive intelligence platform that helps track competitor movements and messaging in real time.

To bring structure to your research, apply a framework like the one outlined in Naresh Malhotra's *Marketing Research: An Applied*

Ideal Strategic Account Profile Worksheet

	Strategic Account Demographics	
1	What is the seniority level and decision-making authority of the key stakeholders within the target account?	
2	Which business units, departments, or functions are most relevant to our value proposition (e.g., IT, Operations, Finance, Procurement)?	
3	What are the organization's top strategic priorities or transformation goals over the next 12–18 months?	
4	How aware is the account of our organization's brand, solutions, and reputation in their industry?	
5	What is the current relationship stage (e.g., awareness, engaged, advocate) with key contacts and the account team?	
6	What critical business or operational challenges does this account face that our solutions can directly address?	
7	How does our offering align with the account's goals, technology roadmap, or sustainability agenda?	
8	What motivates and drives decision makers (e.g., innovation, risk mitigation, efficiency, customer experience, pain points)?	
9	Nice to haves or desired outcomes from external stakeholders?	
10	Insights from sales, partners, account team, or social listening that could inform personalization and engagement?	

Figure 4.2 Ideal Strategic Account Profile Worksheet

Orientation.[13] It emphasizes thoughtful planning, reliable data collection, and rigorous interpretation—ensuring your research is grounded and actionable. I keep a copy of Malhotra's book, Marketing Research: An Applied Orientation on my desk as a reminder of the importance of disciplined inquiry.

But research is only useful if you apply it. The insights you gather should directly inform your ISAP, guide account selection, and shape tailored messaging. When you combine market analysis, competitive intelligence, and structured methodology, you gain a holistic view of where your solution fits—and where it can stand out (Figure 4.2).

This upfront investment sets the tone for everything else. Get it right, and all of your ABM tactics (1:Many, 1:Few, and 1:1) become more in-focus, efficient, and impactful. Get it wrong, and you risk pouring energy and money into the wrong opportunities. In ABM, clarity at the beginning defines success at the end.

[13]Malhotra (2019).

Implementing an Account Nomination Processes

Focusing effort is a fundamental concept, whether you're planning a cross-country trip or building a business. Directing energy toward the most promising avenues makes all the difference. When it comes to identifying those vital client relationships, establishing clear guidelines for choosing strategic accounts is essential. This is about ensuring that the target accounts you prioritize genuinely support company objectives and offer significant upsides. In all ABM efforts, you're looking for value and room to expand, defined by specific, measurable aspects.

Setting the stage for this selection means nailing down precise criteria. What makes an account "*strategic*"? It boils down to several factors for close examination:

- What is the pipeline revenue opportunity? This isn't just current spend but the potential revenue over time.
- Does this account fit with where the company is heading? Consider its fit with your overall business direction and targets.
- What is the chance to build solid relationships with key stakeholders? Understanding key individuals and the possibility of strong connections is a must.
- Does this account hold sway? Think about its standing and capacity to influence trends or ideas.
- What is the potential for growth of the target account? Evaluate its potential for adding more business over time.

Moving from criteria to action requires a defined approach for making selections. A structured nomination process ensures consistency and fairness. This means creating a standard form for proposing accounts, detailing the relevant information. It also involves setting up a clear way to measure nominated accounts against the criteria you've set. Gathering input from individuals across different teams is a critical step here. And a willingness to stick to the defined guidelines and reviewing the selection should red flags appear.

Bringing together people from sales, marketing, and execution provides different viewpoints on an account's potential and the viability of building connections. Their combined insights paint a more complete picture. This is why the Onboarding step in the process is imperative. You are not only educating the account team but also evaluating if they have the necessary desire, understanding and relationships to be selected as a Strategic ABM account.

Finally, revisiting nominations on a regular basis is key to keeping the process sharp. Schedule recurring meetings to look at proposed accounts and check on those already selected. I like to have monthly meetings to update status of all current accounts and revisit what accounts are potentially identified for the future of the program. Continuously tracking account activity and adapting the selection guidelines as needed ensures the process remains effective over time. This also provides you the necessary insights should something change, and you need to quickly move to other potential accounts.

A tool that significantly helps manage this process is a nomination form, either through Microsoft forms or some other tool. Creating a standard template makes submissions uniform, leading to evaluations that are both consistent and quicker. This template should include basic account details like name and industry; estimates of revenue and growth; notes on strategic fit and market standing; and details about key contacts and potential connection strength. Using such a template streamlines things, cutting down on review time and ensuring all necessary information is gathered from the start.

I strongly suggest beginning this process in year three of your program. As you will probably have other issues to align prior to developing a form for account selection. And as stated much earlier, you may choose to develop an Agentic AI Agent to assist you in your selection process to avoid human error.

Prioritization Frameworks for 1:1 Engagement

Think about building something significant. A house, a business, maybe even just a complex meal. You never have infinite time, money, or ingredients. You have to choose where to put your energy. That's the reality for anyone running a targeted marketing effort, especially when you're talking about ABM focused on just a few key targeted accounts. You can't be everywhere for everyone. Being able to tell people NO is a key part of almost any role but more so when you're successful at Strategic ABM.

Choosing who to focus on becomes the first, and maybe the most critical, decision. Getting this wrong means scattering your limited resources onto accounts that won't pay off, leaving the truly valuable ones underserved. Getting it right means directing your focus where it can make the biggest difference, where the return on your effort is highest. This process of selecting your targets isn't just administrative; it's deeply strategic. The need for ABM to have a commanding voice at the table when making these decisions is key to success. I've seen senior leadership select accounts for 1:1 ABM campaigns without discussing them with the ABM team. And these choices have proven to be some of the most costly and unsuccessful decisions that I've seen.

Where to Point the Ship

So, how do you make those choices? It starts not with the accounts themselves, but with looking inward. What does your business need to achieve to be successful? What are the big revenue targets, the key market segments the company is betting on? Your account selection must mirror these broader company aims. Focusing on accounts that are genuinely critical to hitting those goals ensures that your marketing efforts aren't just busywork, but directly contribute to the company's success. Getting leaders onboard with this connection is vital for making sure the approach sticks and can grow. When I started as the head of marketing at Fox Plumbing and Heating, we were spending all of our marketing budget across almost every type of lead generation platform you could imagine. The first thing I did was audit which services were generating the largest margin of profit. I overlaid this information with any changes in market or market trends. Finally, I looked at seasonal changes based on sales to see if there was any correlation between times of the year and increases in specific sales for the company. Once I had this data, I was able to help point the company in the right direction. I canceled the underperforming contracts, restructured our focus on spend and moved from paying third parties for lead generation efforts to developing our own process to drive down costs and increase profit margins.

Sizing Up the Prize

Once you know what kind of accounts fit the plan, you must evaluate their individual worth. How much potential does a specific account hold? This means looking at the possible size of a deal, sure, but also thinking longer term. What's the value of a lasting partnership? Consider what challenges they face right now, what they're trying to achieve. Understanding them helps you see where you fit and the significance of that fit.

Are They Even Listening?

Here's a simple truth: it doesn't matter how perfect an account is on paper if they won't engage with you. Personal relevance demands a realistic look at their willingness to connect. Do they have a history of interacting with your company or industry? Are there existing connections with key people? Do they seem open to exploring new ideas or solutions? Accounts that show signs of being receptive are naturally higher priorities than those that are closed off.

Can You Get Through the Door?

Even if an account is a perfect strategic fit and seems willing to talk, you have to consider the practicalities. Can you realistically build the necessary connections? Think about how they make decisions, who the important people are, and if you have any existing links. Directing your energy where building relationships is feasible is just smart resource management.

Who Else Is Knocking?

Finally, you can't prioritize in a vacuum. Look at who your rivals are within those target accounts. What are they doing? Where are they strong, and where might they be weak? Knowing the competitive environment helps you figure out how to position yourself differently and make your approach stand out.

Getting personal relevance right means constantly revisiting these factors. It's not a one-time exercise. Start with clear business objectives, build a system to judge potential and willingness, consider access, and understand the competition. By doing this consistently, you make sure your ABM efforts are focused on the accounts where they're most likely to generate significant results and build valuable, lasting connections.

Building Consensus and Gaining Stakeholder Buy-In

Projects rarely stall because of poor planning—they stall when people aren't aligned. Think of it like trying to build a house when the architect, contractor, and homeowner can't agree on where the front door should go. For a high-stakes, resource-intensive initiative like Strategic ABM, alignment is the key.

The foundation of that alignment begins with agreeing on which accounts to pursue. That decision can't be made in isolation. sales, marketing, and leadership all bring unique—and necessary—perspectives to the table. Sales teams offer real-world insights from the front lines. Marketing understands growth potential and buyer behavior. Leadership connects the effort to strategic business goals. Bringing everyone together early ensures a well-rounded view and helps build shared ownership of the target list.

Account selection shouldn't feel random—or constrained. It needs to be grounded in **evidence**. Build your case using data: look at market conditions, financial health, and strategic fit. A transparent, analytical approach gives weight to your recommendations and connects account selection directly to broader business outcomes. It's the difference between a gut feeling and a strategic move.

Of course, bringing different teams together means you'll encounter differing opinions—and that's a good thing. Diverse perspectives lead to better decisions, as long as there's a culture that encourages open dialogue. Create space for people to ask questions, raise concerns, and feel heard. Address disagreements early to build trust and avoid roadblocks later.

To keep the process fair and consistent, define clear selection criteria upfront. What makes an account a strong fit? Is it revenue potential, strategic alignment, market position, or something else? Writing these criteria down removes ambiguity and ensures everyone understands the "why" behind each choice (Figure 4.3).

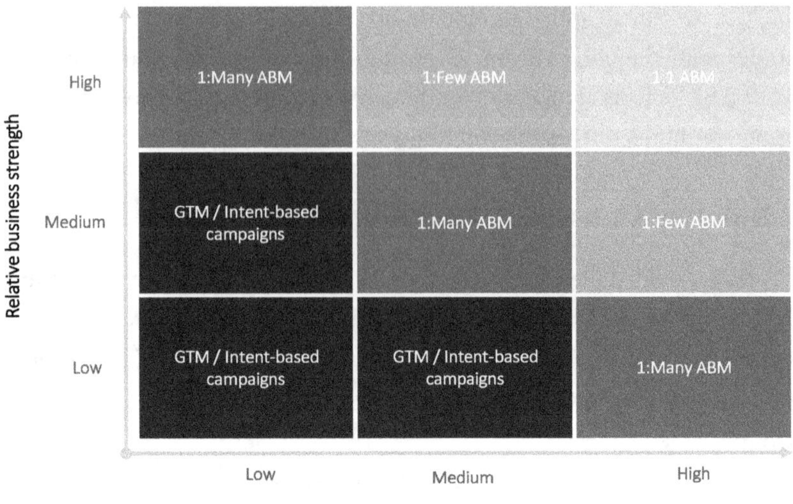

Figure 4.3 Potential ABM account selection

Just as important: document the process. Keep track of which accounts were chosen, why they were chosen, and what discussions shaped those decisions. This record becomes your blueprint for accountability and a reference point for future efforts. As Simon Sinek puts it, "Start with Why."[14] When people understand the purpose behind the list, they're far more likely to rally behind it.

Together, these practices create a solid foundation for Strategic ABM success—one where everyone is aligned in direction, confident in the process, and committed to hitting shared goals.

[14]Sinek (2009).

CHAPTER 5

Deep Account Intelligence and Understanding

Researching Target Accounts

Getting to know a target account requires looking at them from multiple angles. Building a clear picture starts by gathering information that is freely shared. Company publications, reports in the press, details about their industry, and activity on social platforms offer initial views into their operations, priorities, and market standing. While these sources build a crucial first layer of understanding, creating a truly informed view means going further. It means bringing in additional data from outside sources, tapping into the direct experience of your own teams who interact with the account daily, and watching for significant shifts or events that signal change. The process begins with what is openly shared.

Gathering Publicly Available Insights and News

Understanding a target account often feels like piecing together a jigsaw puzzle. Where does one even begin? Much of the initial assembly relies on what's openly shared with the world. This publicly available information forms the base, the necessary starting point before you can even think about adding more detailed pieces. Analyzing these open sources lets you build a foundational grasp of the companies you care about and reveals the areas where you still need to dig deeper.

Consider a potential target account's own website. Think of it as their curated front door, a significant source of knowledge. Here, you find their mission, what drives them, their leadership structure, and details on what matters most to them This material gives you key insight into their purpose, how they see themselves, and what they bring to the market. Looking at their stated mission, for instance, tells you about their core objectives. Their leadership section introduces the individuals steering the ship.

Moving past how the target account sees itself, news releases and articles from the press shine a light on specific actions and events. This allows you to understand how others see them. Product unveilings, agreements with others, acquisitions, financial outcomes—these are reported here. These sources keep you current on their recent moves and help you to bring everything into focus. Studying these accounts helps pinpoint significant turning points, like changes in who's in charge or major financial commitments they've made.

Another tact is reviewing industry news. This provides you with a wider setting. It helps you see where the account sits among competitors and the challenges they face. Keeping up with general trends and happenings in their sector helps clarify their market position and shows potential opportunities and/or risks. This will help you identify both talking and the client's pain points.

For a look at the immediate moment, social media platforms offer real-time glimpses. They allow you to track public sentiment, how people are interacting with the target account, and new trends as they emerge. Watching a target account's presence on these platforms gives you a sense of how their brand is perceived, how customers are engaging, and how the target account views itself and understands their culture. This is also extremely helpful when developing imagery for collateral that resonates down the road.

Putting these sources together allows you to form a substantial understanding of your potential target account and shows where more focused investigation is needed. This process helps identify key decision makers, grasp the company's goals and hurdles, build a more detailed picture of their offerings, and shape your strategy for how to connect with them to build partnerships.

In summary, here are a few best practices worth keeping in mind: Regularly check sites, news releases, and articles. Use tools that listen to social media conversations to monitor sentiment and engagement. Analyze broader industry movements to grasp the market setting. Utilizing these open resources provides a strong basis for understanding and prepares for diving deeper later.

Remember, you may not be able to do all of this for every target account you are looking to onboard. Doing parts or even a pass of all of these will help to put you in a much better position as you proceed down the Strategic ABM path.

Utilizing Third-Party Data Sources and Intent Signals

Imagine trying to get to know someone, but only looking at their shopping list from your store. You'd know what they bought from you, but you'd miss everything else. Their hobbies, their job, their favorite teams, other vendors they purchase from, what they're thinking about right now—all hidden. This is too often the situation when businesses rely solely on their internal data to grasp their most important accounts. What you have in your customer system or CRM platform tells a story, but it's only part of the epic tale.

To really get a grip on what matters to these accounts, you need information that comes from outside your organization. Bringing in third-party data offers details your internal records simply don't have. Think of it as adding chapters to your target account's story, providing context and color that makes your efforts to engage them, particularly in ABM, much more meaningful. Moving past the limitations of your own data lets you see a much clearer, more detailed picture of who you're trying to reach.

Finding the right external data is crucial, naturally. You need sources that specialize in information specific to the industries your target accounts are in, or data related to their actual operations. These are vendors who can provide insights into account actions, what they prefer, and the challenges they face. When you're looking, there are a few things that are absolute musts:

- **Tailoring to the Need**: Make certain the data applies directly to the accounts you care about and fits with how you plan to approach them.
- **Being on Target:** Double-click on the data to ensure accuracy. Take the time to dig a bit and make sure the data is correct. Making decisions based on wrong information is worse than having no information at all.

- **Seeing Everything All at Once:** Look for sources that offer a wide view—details about the company itself (firmographic), the technology they use (technographic), and what they are actively researching (**intent**).

That last one, **intent data**, is particularly insightful. It shows you the subjects and areas accounts are researching online right now. This gives you a real-time window into what's occupying their thoughts and what they might need. Using this kind of data helps you spot accounts that are showing clear signs of desire to engage with you. It allows you to adjust your outreach based on what you know they're thinking about today and helps guide their experience from their first engagement through to becoming a valued partner. Applying intent data means you can craft interactions that feel highly personal and relevant to the specific accounts you're engaging.

While intent data is powerful by itself, its true strength comes when you combine it with additional insight. This means putting intent data alongside your internal records and other industry knowledge. This builds a more complete picture of a target account's needs and what they find to be important.

- Craft approaches that directly speak to what each account is interested in.
- Increase the chances of engagement success because you are reaching out to them first with solutions.
- Build better relationships with target accounts by showing you truly understand their situation and priorities.

Deepening your understanding of accounts with external data allows you to build a richer, more detailed view of them. This directly leads to ABM strategies that work better and show improved conversion rates.

Gleaning Insights from Account Teams

Think about the best sources of information about the people you want to reach. Often, the most insightful details aren't hidden in complex market reports or competitor analysis. They're right there, walking the halls, sitting in meetings, answering questions in Microsoft Teams. Your own people—the ones talking to accounts every day—know things. They possess a wealth of knowledge and understanding about your target accounts, knowledge built through countless daily interactions and ongoing connections.

Sales teams, for example, sit closest to an account's strategic aims, its immediate concerns, and who they're currently and potentially considering working with. This perspective is fundamental to grasping what an account genuinely needs and shaping how you should approach. Service or Execution team members, on the other hand, see how customers use your product, where they find value, and where there might be unmet needs. Their view shows the account's current experience. The team as a whole is tasked with overseeing the entire health of the account, each part serves a vital role in bringing everything into focus for the ABMer. By integrating what sales sees, what service hears, and what account management understands, businesses can develop a higher resolution picture of an account—their struggles, their aspirations, and their desires.

But how do you get this understanding out of individual heads and into a place where everyone can access? It requires setting up ways for knowledge to flow freely. You need feedback loops. This means creating a process to gather and share the insights these teams hold, preventing valuable details from staying isolated or getting lost in the shuffle. Doing this systematically helps pinpoint critical account aims and difficulties, clarify satisfaction levels and missing requirements, provide a complete picture of the relationship's standing, and directly inform and strengthen marketing plans directed at specific accounts.

One of the most effective methods is conducting structured interviews or positioning calls. Talking to internal teams with a clear set of questions can reveal vital intelligence for account strategies. These conversations offer rich, descriptive data. You can identify key decision makers and their functions, grasp account objectives and obstacles, develop messaging that speaks directly to them, and improves how effective your focused marketing efforts are. You can also use these opportunities to develop positioning for messaging.

Now that you're armed with the internal knowledge, you can blend the internal insights with your external research. This combination helps validate assumptions, uncover blind spots, and round out understanding. The result is a more accurate and actionable view of the target account—one that supports sharper, more strategic decision making.

By pairing your team's firsthand experience with external market signals, media perception, and public sentiment, you can craft more effective strategies and avoid costly missteps. This well-rounded approach should always inform your ABM account selection process.

For example, in the fall of 2024, we considered adding a major health insurance provider based in Minnesota to our Strategic ABM program. Internally, the account looked promising—existing relationships were strong, and initial engagement was positive. But then, a high-profile tragedy occurred, significantly shifting public sentiment toward the company. Because we were actively monitoring external perception, we quickly recognized the reputational risk and made the decision to pause the Onboarding process. Had we relied solely on internal signals, we likely would have moved forward—potentially jeopardizing both the program's credibility and long-term success of the Strategic ABM program.

This experience reinforced a simple truth: A complete picture requires looking both inwardly, outwardly, and regularly. In ABM, context is everything.

Understanding the Account's Business Challenges, Goals, and Initiatives

You wouldn't build a strategy to reach someone without understanding what drives them, what keeps them up at night, or what outcomes they're looking for. That basic understanding of the target account is the ground floor for anything effective you want to do in Strategic ABM. It's where you find the challenges and goals that matter, shaping everything that follows in marketing and sales. If you ask the right question today, they will listen to you tomorrow.

How do you start framing your picture? First, look outward. Use what's already public knowledge. Think of it as gathering your observation clues first.

Review their annual reports. These documents aren't just about numbers; they lay out where the company has been, what big moves they intended to make, and how they see their own progress. They talk about strategic aims and major achievements, giving you a sense of their priorities straight from the source.

And consider their investor presentations if you can find recordings. Here, executives often speak more plainly about performance, what they expect next, and where they plan to invest their energy and money. This gives you a chance to hear where they are steering the ship in their own words.

We've discussed this at length earlier, but you should always speak with your internal teams.

Building this detailed picture will move you past assumptions and toward a targeted ABM approach that truly addresses the account's unique situation and objectives. With this groundwork, creating content, messages, and engagement plans that genuinely connect becomes much clearer and more effective. Now, you're ready to aim precisely at your target account.

Identifying Key Triggers and Opportunity Signals

Standing still is rarely an option in business, especially for these high-value accounts you're looking at onboarding in Strategic ABM. Their world isn't static; it's shaped by forces often outside their immediate control. Understanding these external forces is essential. These shifts alter needs, redefine what matters most, and change circumstances in ways that create opportunities for those who are watching closely.

Think about what happens when an industry gets turned on its head, like how Agentic AI is currently changing landscapes. Technological advances, shifts in what customers want/expect, or even surprising new competitors can completely upend established ways of doing things. Industry disruption compels businesses to find new methods and new tools simply to stay competitive. They might have to look hard at their current approach and the vendors they rely on. This is precisely when an ABMer should step in, offering fresh perspectives and creative answers to these evolving opportunities.

Consider the tremors that run through an organization when mergers and acquisitions (M&A) occur. M&A activity injects uncertainty and often triggers a review of existing vendor agreements. When companies combine or one buys another, they assess their current technology and service providers to ensure they fit with the combined entity's future direction. This period of assessment provides a chance for account managers to demonstrate the value their solutions bring and perhaps secure new business within the newly formed organization.

And then there's the simple, human factor of change in leadership. When a new executive takes the helm, they often arrive with different ideas and a willingness to challenge the status quo. New leaders may be more open to hearing about innovative solutions and exploring new business relationships than the old guard. This change can open doors for account managers to grow footprints and introduce concepts and offerings that previous leadership was unwilling to consider.

Spotting these types of shifts—industry disruption, M&A, financial changes, new leaders—allows for proactive engagement with your accounts. It allows you to anticipate how their needs and priorities might change. Armed with this foresight, you can develop targeted solutions that directly address the new challenges they face. Engaging with the relevant stakeholders at the account becomes more impactful when you can speak directly to their current reality, offering value and strengthening your connection. It positions you not just as a vendor but as a thought leader who understands their pains and can offer guidance.

A foundational approach in effective account management involves establishing core messaging themes that guide all future interactions and materials. This method ensures your communication is consistent and addresses the account's specific circumstances and what matters most to them. By aligning your message and what you offer with the account's objectives and obstacles, you can identify significant opportunities that demonstrate your understanding of their business ecosystem.

By grasping these external elements and recognizing the triggers they create, account managers can approach their accounts with purpose. Offering solutions that hit the mark and building solid connections becomes the path to staying ahead and driving expansion through focused account management.

Mapping Stakeholders and Building Personas

Selling into complex organizations requires a precise understanding of the people who shape purchasing outcomes. It's rarely a single individual making the call; instead, a group participates in the decision. Identifying everyone involved, from those with official titles to individuals whose influence stems from expertise or internal connections, is essential. Discovering how these individuals interact, what matters most to them, and how internal factors affect decisions provides the foundation for targeted outreach. Being able to create impactful messaging to these central figures, their perspectives, and motivations moves past broad assumptions and allows for true engagement and the development of relationships.

Identifying the Decision-Making Unit and Influencers

Trying to sell into a complex organization can feel like navigating a labyrinth without a map. You might think you know who holds the purse strings or makes the final call, but often, the reality is far more intricate. It's rarely just one person. Instead, a group of individuals that typically participates in the buying decision for a specific product or service. This group is what we call the Decision-Making Unit, or DMU. Getting a solid handle on who is in this group and how they interact is often the difference between success and spinning your wheels.

To begin piecing together this puzzle, start with the obvious: the organization chart. Mapping the formal roles gives you the skeletal structure. You need to understand the reporting lines and the main duties assigned to each position. This helps identify the obvious players—the people whose titles suggest they should be involved in decisions about what you offer. Consider a company looking to purchase new business software. The people with official roles like CIO, head of IT, or even the chief executive officer might be listed right there on paper as having a say.

Looking only at titles can be like missing the forest for the trees. Beyond the formal structure exist individuals who might not have "Decision Maker" in their job description but carry significant weight. These are the informal influencers. Their impact stems from their technical knowledge, their long-standing relationships within the company, or simply the respect they've earned from colleagues. Think about a senior engineer who deeply understands the technical requirements, or a longtime team lead whose opinion is highly valued by management. Their informal backing—or opposition—can significantly sway how your organization is seen.

Understanding who talks to whom, and what subjects frequently come up in those conversations, reveals connections and priorities that aren't visible on any chart. This analysis can show you which stakeholders interact most often, what their common concerns are, and where potential alignments or conflicts might exist regarding a purchase like yours. Perhaps the operations team constantly discusses efficiency needs with the finance department; knowing this helps you understand their shared interests.

With the various individuals identified, it will become clear that not everyone holds the same amount of sway. It's necessary to sort these key stakeholders by their level of influence and how much direct authority they have over the decision. Focusing your energy on those who can champion your solution, or block it, ensures you're applying resources where they will have the most impact. Concentrating efforts on a key champion can move things forward much faster than trying to persuade someone with minimal involvement.

To truly understand the people you need to engage, connect the formal roles with the informal influence. See how the official structure interacts with the unofficial network. Analyze what drives each person—their specific needs, their interests, and any potential biases they might have. Building detailed profiles, or personas, for these individuals allows you to see them not just as job titles but as people with distinct perspectives. This deep understanding allows for a more thoughtful approach.

Knowing the DMU down to this level enables you to craft specific ways to interact with each key person. This involves creating messages, content, and experiences designed to resonate with their individual perspectives and priorities. In Strategic ABM, this level of personal relevance is essential. It helps build trust and establish credibility because you are speaking directly to their world, their challenges, and their goals. This targeted engagement increases the likelihood of achieving a positive outcome.

In a recent strategic account that I worked on, we found that providing platforms to senior leadership to showcase our thought leadership was imperative to opening doors and finding senior leadership advocates. We invited leaders to come and speak at multiple global sales kick-off meetings and client account briefings. These small things will make major differences in your relationship with the account.

Understanding Individual Roles, Responsibilities, and Politics

Getting through to people, and making them stop and think, feels like the whole point of marketing. It's not enough just to know who's who and who you need to connect with. You must grasp what makes them tick and how they see the world from their seat at the table. This is fundamental when you're aiming for focused growth. Without it, you're just shouting into the void, hoping someone hears you.

Identifying the main decision makers, the people who might sway their opinion, and anyone who could potentially slow things down is your first step in creating relationships in ABM. Getting this roadmap right early on helps teams drive your efforts to where they'll have the most impact. Imagine knowing that the person holding the budget is the VP of marketing, but the team that uses your product day-to-day, led by the director of sales operations, has a say in the final decision. Your strategy should focus on the director based on this insight.

A job title is just the cover of the book. To really get it, you need to understand what fills their day. What are their daily tasks? What are their biggest worries? How is their own success measured? When you know a stakeholder's main aim is, you can speak directly to how your offering helps them achieve that. It makes your message instantly more relevant.

Then there are the hidden currents—the informal ways people interact and influence each other. These can be just as powerful as the official organizational chart. Sometimes, the person with the most influence isn't the one with the highest title. It's the guy with the best shoes. Finding these informal champions, or even identifying potential points of resistance you didn't expect, requires looking beyond the obvious. This layer of understanding allows for engagement that respects the real dynamics at play.

Communication preferences matter too. Do they like quick e-mails, or do they prefer a detailed PowerPoint presentation? Do they appreciate a direct approach, or a more subtle one? Adapting how you talk to someone helps build trust and makes them more receptive to what you have to say. It's about connecting on their terms.

All of this insight—their official standing, their daily work, their unofficial influence, and their communication style—becomes your foundation for how you craft messages and plan your interactions. You become more effective when you can speak directly to the specific worries and goals of each individual you're trying to reach. This could involve crafting tailored outreach or positioning your solution in a way that resonates deeply with specific individuals or groups within the account.

Knowing the individuals for a target account—their roles, their duties, and the internal dynamics—isn't just helpful; it's essential for success in targeted growth strategies. It allows teams to build stronger connections, have more meaningful discussions, and find new possibilities for growth.

Creating Detailed Account Personas for Key Individuals

Think about the last time someone truly understood you. It makes a difference in how you do business with them, doesn't it? It shifts the conversation from generic noise to something that actually connects. In the world of ABM, achieving that level of connection within target accounts requires a similar depth of understanding. This is where crafting detailed account personas becomes less of a task and more of a necessity. It's the way we take raw data—the names, the job titles, the company details—and breathe life into it, turning impersonal statistics into relatable profiles of real individuals.

Why do this? Because Strategic ABM is like your short game in golf. Traditional marketing gets you close but ABM helps put it on the green with customized engagement with the individuals who matter most. To engage effectively, you need to know who they are, not just what they are.

Getting to know these individuals starts, as many things do, with some focused detective work. You need to research their backgrounds and understand their professional paths. Platforms like LinkedIn are obvious starting points, offering glimpses into their roles and connections.

Company websites and industry publications add layers, revealing their company's priorities and their own contributions. This investigation isn't just collecting facts; it's gathering clues to understand their professional history and current position.

A few years ago, we were leading a live demonstration on how to build effective ABM campaigns for a room full of marketers. The case study focused on a major national bank in South Africa. The room immediately dove into stakeholder mapping—analyzing reporting structures, debating the best path to engage mid-level managers, and working through a top-down engagement sequence.

As I looked closer at the C-suite, something stood out: almost every senior leader had earned their MBA from Harvard. A quick bit of research confirmed that many of them also subscribed to the *Harvard Business Review* podcast.

That was my aha moment.

Rather than spending time and resources navigating the layers of the org chart, I suggested we go straight to the source. We proposed placing our message where they were already actively engaged—through a sponsorship or strategic placement on the very podcast they were already listening to. In one move, we bypassed the complexity and reached our tier-one audience in a context they trusted and respected.

This lesson is simple but powerful: don't always climb the ladder—sometimes you can take the elevator. Strategic ABM isn't just about mapping influence; it's about recognizing behavioral signals and meeting decision makers where they already are.

Another critical piece of the puzzle is figuring out where they sit in the account's decision-making structure. Mapping their influence within the company unit, understanding their preferred communication channels, and knowing what sources of information they trust are all essential. These insights help you figure out the most effective ways to reach them and ensure your message is delivered in a way that resonates with their specific needs and how they process information.

Once you've gathered all these pieces—the background, the role analysis, the understanding of their challenges, goals, motivations, and influence—you can build detailed and nuanced personas. These aren't just basic profiles; they capture the essence of each person. They include their professional journey, their key objectives, the obstacles they face, and how they like to communicate. Having these rich personas is the foundation for developing targeted engagement strategies that connect deeply with the individuals you want to reach.

As you build these personas, there are a few things worth keeping in mind. First, establish a core set of messaging pillars—maybe three foundational themes—that everything you say or do will revolve around when engaging this persona. Think about how personal branding works; communicating identity and value before the main interaction sets the stage. Apply that thinking here. And critically, these aren't static documents. Keep your personas updated and refined as you gather new information or as circumstances within the account change.

Following these principles helps you create accurate, actionable personas that drive personalized engagement and build stronger connections with your audience. It requires effort, certainly, but the return in meaningful engagement and improved outcomes makes it a worthwhile pursuit. It's how we move from marketing to an account to connecting with the people who inhabit it.

Mapping Relationships and Networks Within the Account

When we talk about Strategic ABM, focusing on the outside is the natural instinct. Who are the target accounts? What are their pain points? What are their budgets? But often, the real puzzle isn't just what they need, but how they decide they need it. It turns out, understanding the inside of a company—the human connections and power lines—matters just as much, sometimes more, than understanding the market outside.

Think about it. Every company, large or small, is a collection of people working together, or sometimes, not quite together. Decisions don't happen in a vacuum or solely because a single person has a title. They happen through conversations, recommendations, approvals, and sometimes quiet disagreements. Getting a handle on this involves looking past the official organizational chart. It means figuring out the true dynamic of "who's who" inside that account.

This isn't just corporate gossip; it's essential intelligence. Knowing these connections reveals where influence truly lies. It shows you who listens to whom, who respects whose opinion, and who might be able to smooth the path or accidentally throw a stick in your spoke. With the correct insight, you can refine your approach, aiming your message not just at the right department but at the people who actually sway opinions and greenlight initiatives. You can spot the champions who will advocate for you and the potential hurdles you'll need to address.

One practical way to make sense of this complex picture is by visualizing it. Drawing out a map of the company, marking down individuals and the lines connecting them—formal reporting lines, yes, but also informal connections. This mapping process helps make the invisible visible, showing clearly who the likely proponents or opponents might be when it comes to considering a new product or service. This visual guide then informs exactly how you should approach different individuals, making your outreach far more likely to connect.

Certain individuals stand out in these internal networks: the connectors. These are the people who don't just stay in their lane; they have friends, colleagues, and contacts across different departments. They are the bridges that span the silos. Getting to know and engage with these connectors can be incredibly valuable. These are the people who, more than likely, your account team deals with daily. And that's why their involvement and insight is invaluable.

All of this information—who knows who, who the connectors are, what hidden groups exist—comes together in relationship maps. These maps become working documents, detailing the intricate network within the account. They serve as a practical guide, allowing you to personalize your interactions. Instead of a generic pitch, you can tailor your communication and engagement based on the specific relationships and influence points you've identified. This targeted interaction is much more effective at building genuine relationships.

Bringing it all together, the structures and people within companies aren't static. People move roles, leave, or new ones join. Relationships shift. What was true yesterday might not be today. For this reason, keeping these relationship maps updated is essential. Regularly reviewing and refining will ensure that your understanding remains up to date. An outdated map is like using a GPS in 2010—you might be OK, but you could also end up driving into a pond. Keeping them current ensures your strategies remain relevant and effective, adapting as the target account itself changes internally.

Once you've done all of this then you'll find that your maps will help you navigate the labyrinth of who to talk to and when in your journey of developing your Strategic ABM campaigns.

Understanding Individual Pain Points, Motivations, and Communication Styles

In marketing, sharing general messages that might land somewhere in the crowd is easy. But reaching individuals, understanding what makes them nervous, that requires a different kind of focus.

This is where ABM, especially the Strategic ABM specialization, truly shines. The starting point for that conversation? Getting a handle on their specific needs and hurdles. Think of it like figuring out what problem someone needs solved before you even start talking about your solution. As my father used to say, "What do you want us to do?"

Finding What Hurts

In weekly ABM calls we regularly discuss "pain points," and it's a useful term. It simply means the specific issues or challenges a potential customer is grappling with—things your product or service is built to fix. In Strategic ABM, you're not just guessing at common industry problems. You're zeroing in on the troubles specific people face within a target account. This focus allows for engagement that's intensely personal, making sure your proposed fixes aren't just relevant to the target account as a whole, but also speak directly to the individual's concerns. It helps make sure your offers connect with the exact worries of the person you're trying to build a relationship with.

How do you discover what troubles you're having? There's no one method that fits all; it's a mixed bag. You'll need to do a bit of active listening:

- **Listening on Social Media:** Pay attention to what people are discussing online. What challenges related to their job or industry do they mention? If you have a Sales Navigator account, you can follow and set alerts for your DMU audience.

- **Surveys and Client Conversation:** Sometimes the simplest way is best. Ask. Surveys can gather broader feedback, while one-on-one conversations utilizing qualitative laddering techniques can provide deeper understanding. If you can, get invited to regular client meetings or quarterly reviews. This will provide you massive insights that the account team may not pick up on.
- **Understand your Account:** Look at data you have already accumulated. A great free tool for external insights is Google Trends. You can automate it to do regular pulls of news relating to your target accounts. This not only keeps you informed but can make you invaluable to the account team. What do you know about the target account? What about the individuals within it?
- **People Mapping:** Figure out who the key players are inside the target account. What are their jobs? What responsibilities do they carry? What might their priorities be? Understanding their role gives clues to their potential challenges.

Always Make it Personal

Once you have a handle on what's bothering your target audience you can adapt how you communicate your solutions.

- **Content, a Combination of Personalized and Customized:** Create materials that speak directly to the problems you've identified. This shows you've been listening and understanding their world.
- **Solutions Shaped to Fit:** Round pegs go in round holes. Offer solutions that are designed with their unique challenges in mind. Generic offers don't work; it's about providing something specific that helps your key stakeholder.
- **Engagement Where They Are:** Reach out using the methods and formats they prefer. This makes sure your message is not only heard but also received in a way that feels natural to them.

Why This Works

Focusing on individual pain points brings several clear advantages:

- **Better Engagement:** When your approach feels personal and relevant, people pay more attention. They see you understand them.
- **Higher Success Rates:** Solutions that solve specific problems are much more likely to be accepted. You're offering a direct fix to something they care about.
- **Stronger Relationships:** Showing you understand someone's difficulties builds trust and helps create more meaningful connections over time.

Staying Sharp

This isn't a one-time task. To keep your 1:1 ABM campaigns effective, you need to be constantly listening. Continually getting feedback on key stakeholder worries helps you adapt and improve your approach over time.

- **Chat on the Regular:** Schedule interactions to catch up, gather feedback, and learn about new challenges as they come up.
- **Build Feedback Systems:** Make it easy for people to share their thoughts on your solutions and engagement techniques.

Putting the effort into identifying individual challenges and staying responsive to their needs allows businesses to build effective Strategic ABM strategies. This focus helps boost engagement and conversion rates and contributes to a customer experience that feels genuinely personal and impactful.

CHAPTER 6

Crafting the Bespoke Account Experience

You're going to like the way you look. I guarantee it.

George Zimmer, Men's Wearhouse[15]

Developing Content and Messaging That Makes an Impact

Customization isn't about dropping someone's first name into a mass e-mail. That's not bespoke marketing—that's automation with a thin disguise. Reaching high-value accounts effectively requires more than messaging. It requires understanding.

As we've explored, research plays a crucial role in identifying a target account's objectives, challenges, and market dynamics. From those insights, your next step is to shape a strong, concise value proposition. In essence, your value prop should clearly answer: *Why us? Why now?* It should directly connect your solution—whether it's a service, product, or platform—to the account's specific pain points and strategic priorities.

An effective value proposition will do these three things well:

- They map your solution to the account's unique challenges.
- They quantify potential outcomes or business value.
- They deliver messaging in a tone and format that resonates with the account's audience.

When executed correctly, your content stops feeling like marketing and starts feeling like a solution with true value. It becomes targeted, timely, and relevant—building trust and prompting action.

---

[15]Zimmer (1998).

Great ABM is about transforming generic outreach into meaningful dialogue. That only happens when you deeply understand your audience and speak to their world—not yours.

Tailoring Value Propositions to Account Needs and Goals

We all talk about the importance of connection in business—the idea that understanding who you're speaking to changes everything. It sounds obvious. Yet, how often do we still see generic communication flood inboxes and pitch meetings? The one-size-fits-all deck. The impersonal e-mail. The gap between knowing we should personalize and actually doing it remains far too wide—especially when engaging high-value accounts.

Your goal is to craft something that doesn't just arrive—it resonates. Something that doesn't just get read—but remembered.

It all starts with understanding what truly drives the account. What are their big-picture objectives? Their strategic imperatives? 'Never ask a question you don't know the answer to' is an old legal adage that serves you well here. Go beyond the surface: study their mission statement, leadership commentary, investor presentations, or sustainability pledges. Understand how they frame success internally. This allows you to frame your solution in a way that aligns with their aspirations from the outset. When you speak their language, you show respect—and credibility.

I'll never forget what Stuart Wilson, then CEO of MS&L, told me once, "Of all the things you can get wrong when working on an account, you can't ever get their name wrong." Because if you mess up the basics—like a name—you're showing the client they're not worth the effort. And if that's the message you send before you've even made a case for value, you've already lost the opportunity.

Beyond stated goals, you must dig into where the friction lies. Every organization has challenges. You need to take your research during your account selection process and put it to use here. Where are they struggling? What internal or market pressures are slowing them down? You've already compiled the data, now you need to fold it into your messaging. Explore their competitive landscape. Who's gaining ground on them? Where do they lag behind their peers? What macroeconomic or industry changes are they likely contending with? The more nuanced your picture, the more relevant your content will be.

This is why ABM spends so much time understanding the target accounts' challenges because the next step is bridging them directly to your solution. This isn't about rattling off product features. That's what Branding is for. This is about how your offering solves a specific bottleneck, reduces a known cost, or helps provide an advantage in their market? Think of it as building a bridge from their current pain to their desired state—with your solution as their path forward.

Personal relevance alone isn't enough. You also need to quantify the impact. Business decisions are rarely made without numbers. Can you estimate the ROI? Provide a before-and-after case study? Use benchmarks to showcase time saved, revenue gained, or risk reduced? The more you can tie your value to measurable outcomes, the more compelling your proposition becomes—especially to decision makers in finance, operations, or the C-suite.

One key option that I have found is that on-site workshops go a long way to understanding the account. You have a face-to-face opportunity to have your key leadership in the room with their key decision makers and create an opportunity for deeper relationships and broader understanding of the Strategic ABM account's needs.

All of this culminates in crafting a message that feels like it was made for them—because it was. A message that reflects their goals, acknowledges their struggles, speaks their language, and offers a concrete path forward. Use terms and examples familiar to their industry. Cite competitors or market conditions they're aware of. Focus your message on the benefits that matter most to them.

When done well, a combination of personalized and customer tailored value proposition doesn't just stand out—it fits in. It feels like an extension of the account's own strategic thinking. And when that happens, the conversation shifts from, "Why should we talk to you?" to "How soon can we get started?"

Creating Account-Specific Content Assets (Case Studies, Proposals, Reports)

Connecting with people, really connecting, often feels like finding a unique frequency only they can understand. In the business world, particularly when we're talking about the accounts that matter most, the need to connect isn't just nice; it's fundamental. ABM pushes us to move past broad messages and focus on tuning into those individual frequencies. It asks us to craft messages and materials that land squarely with the needs of specific, highly valued accounts. This starts with truly getting inside their world—understanding their company, the sector they operate in, and the hurdles they face day-to-day. When we do this, the content we create speaks right to their situation, building connections and moving things forward.

Getting this understanding means digging for details. Talking to key people at the account, sending out questions, or simply paying attention to what they're discussing online—these methods help uncover those specific concerns. Once we know their challenges, we can shape our content to show exactly how we can help them clear those obstacles. We demonstrate how working with us translates into tangible benefits.

Think about case studies. They work because they tell a story of success. But they work best in ABM when that story looks a lot like the account's own story. A case study about a manufacturing company overcoming supply chain issues will feel far more real and convincing to another manufacturing company facing similar roadblocks. Mirroring your target account's industry and circumstances builds belief that you understand their world and have the best solution.

Proposals serve a similar purpose but in a more direct way. They are the moment you lay out how you can specifically address the issues you've identified. A strong proposal in Deal Acceleration or Strategic ABM isn't generic; it uses familiar language to the account and points to examples or situations relevant to them. It shows clear ways that will show them why you are the team that provides the solution.

Reports are another way to showcase that what your 1:1 ABM campaign has been promising, your team is able to successfully execute. By providing information and analysis based on solid data, while showing unique insights. A report looking at shifts in their industry or comparing performance metrics within that sector can provide valuable perspective. It shows you're not just selling something but that you're a source of useful knowledge about their business environment.

Putting all this together involves creating actual content—articles, videos, audio clips, or social media updates—designed for a single target account (1:1), or a small group of accounts (1:Few), in mind. This tailored approach creates a personalized experience for them, showing that you've done your homework and are focused on their needs. By making content that feels personal and relevant, we boost interest, encourage action, and ultimately, help businesses grow.

Speaking the Same Language, or Standardizing Messaging Across All Channels

With so much noise, competition, and content overload, ABM success hinges not just on *who* you reach but *how* you speak to them. Being conscious of this is what allows your message to rise above the rest and resonate with the people who matter.

When you tailor your communication to a specific account or key stakeholder, you immediately boost the chances of being heard and, more importantly, remembered. This is more than using a name in a subject line—it's retargeting audiences using technology to capture their intent on your site or creating targeted LinkedIn campaigns to employees at a specific level within your target audience. It's always strange at how well B2C marketing has adapted to this new landscape and how slow B2B marketing has been to adopt these techniques.

Communicating clearly is key when executing your content. I learned this firsthand on a train in Germany, where I experienced a moment of miscommunication that stuck with me. It reminded me that if the person you're speaking to doesn't understand your message, *nothing else matters*. In marketing, clarity and connection start with insight. By leveraging account specific data—how a company behaves, what they value, where they're feeling pressure—this allows you to craft messaging that doesn't just inform but connects. This level of personal relevance drives higher engagement, stronger conversion rates, and ultimately, greater ROI.

Effective messaging isn't just about what you say—it's also about *where* you say it.

Take the classic AdWeek example, "How Do You Advertise to an Ad Agency? Put Up a Billboard Right Across the Street."[16] Intridea, a software design firm, wanted to get the attention of Ogilvy & Mather. They bought a billboard directly across from Ogilvy's New York office with a simple message: "Ogle this, Ogilvy." It was bold, perfectly placed, and impossible to ignore. I loved it because it echoed the same thinking behind my own Krispy Kreme campaign—take a risk, be smart, and go straight at the target in a way your audience can't miss.

The takeaway? Personalization and customization aren't just about message *content*—it's about how you tie the message together and present it.

At the same time, this shouldn't come at the cost of brand consistency. While your tone, content, and channel may vary based on the individual or account, your **brand voice** should remain consistent. That consistency builds recognition and trust, reinforcing what your brand stands for across every channel—from e-mail and social media to direct mail and live events.

And neither personalization or customization is a "set it and forget it" strategy. It's a living, evolving process. What works today may fall flat tomorrow. Regularly test different formats, phrasings, visuals, and delivery methods. Track performance across channels. Refine based on results.

The best Strategic ABM strategies aren't perfect—they're adaptive.

To message effectively across all communication channels, keep these principles in mind:

- **Develop modular content.** Content that's easy to adapt for specific roles, industries, or account situations—templates, decks, case studies, e-mail frameworks, and microsites.
- **Use data to drive messaging.** Let insights guide your strategy—behavioral signals, engagement history, firmographics, and intent data should all inform your messaging.
- **Tailor by channel.** The same message won't work the same way everywhere. Adapt tone and delivery for e-mail, LinkedIn, executive outreach, and direct mail.
- **Protect your brand voice.** You should never make your messaging feel fragmented or off brand. Stay anchored in your brand identity.

---

[16]Adweek Staff (2018).

- **Continuously optimize.** A/B test your subject lines, calls to action, formats, and visuals. Learn what resonates—and evolve with your audience.

Personalization and customization becomes more than tactics - they become differentiators. It shows your target accounts that you're not just marketing *at* them but engaging *with* them.

And in ABM, that kind of relevance is what turns a message into a conversation—and a conversation into a relationship.

Leveraging Account Insights to Create Customized Content

When you have effective communication then it feels like a smooth engine running beneath everything successful in ABM, especially when you're working with a single targeted account. That level of knowledge and understanding, as discussed earlier, will assist you in ensuring your content has personal relevance and is on topic.

Think about trying to have a meaningful conversation with someone you've just met. You wouldn't just rattle off facts about yourself, would you? You'd listen, you'd try to understand their perspective. It's exactly the same with Strategic ABM. You need to speak directly to your audience's individual requirements with carefully crafted messages. This means really understanding their current situation—the state of their industry, who they compete with, what internal projects they have going on.

Gathering what you need to know about an account can happen in several ways. You might talk to key people within the company, listen to what's being said about them online, or get feedback from your sales team who interact with them daily. This is where you will take everything you gathered to date and use it to shape the content you create. This ensures what you put out is relevant right now, arrives at the right moment, and offers real value to the account. Picture crafting a sequence of messages just for a specific audience within your target account. Each message builds on the one before, adding layers of insight, sharing examples of success, offering thoughtful perspectives, and presenting ideas tailored to their specific needs—or creating a "This Then That" (IFTTT) e-mail automation process that when someone clicks on a specific link within an e-mail, they are then taken out of the mainstream of the e-mail and diverted to a distributary that serves them content related to what they clicked on in the e-mail.

Once you start communicating, it's not a one-and-done situation. You constantly look at how your messages are received. Things like whether e-mails get opened, if people click on links, or if you get responses—these tell you if you're hitting the mark. Looking at these engagement signals helps you continuously refine and improve what you're saying to make sure it stays relevant and keeps connecting. Seeing when key individuals are interacting with your content gives you real-time clues about their interest and can open the door for reaching out in a timely and more significant way.

What helps make communication truly effective in 1:1 ABM? A few guiding points come to mind:

Do your homework: Dig deep into the account's difficulties, what they want to achieve, and their industry. Effective and clear communication is the engine that powers successful 1:1 ABM. When it's working well, it feels seamless—like everything is in sync beneath the surface. That level of precision doesn't happen by accident. It requires deep insight into the account and intentional application of what you know.

Develop account team relationships: Stop and listen to your target account. The more you understand your account's unique context—their industry trends, competitors, strategic priorities, and internal initiatives—the more relevant and meaningful your communication becomes.

You can't develop client relationships with a quick Google search. They are built over time and through multiple channels:

- Direct conversations with internal stakeholders
- Feedback from your sales team
- Online behavior and digital engagement signals

- Market insight from tools like Omdia, Klue, Forrester, Gartner, and others
- Industry reports, social listening, and earned media analysis

Once you've collected relevant information, the next step is shaping it into content that matters—right now. That could mean building a series of messages for a specific stakeholder group, where each communication builds upon the last: layering insight, sharing relevant success stories, and offering solutions tied to their challenges.

Or it could mean designing a smart automation journey. For example, if a contact clicks on a link in your e-mail, that action might trigger a tailored follow-up journey—delivering content aligned to their demonstrated interest. If integrated with your ABM advertising platform, it might also increase their engagement or intent score and serve them targeted ads as part of a retargeting strategy. When done well, these systems feel seamless and personal—not automated.

Equally important, where you communicate:

- Different stakeholders live on different platforms. Some accounts may be most responsive to e-mail. Others might favor LinkedIn, in-person events, industry forums, CABs—or, occasionally, a well-placed digital or physical advert. The more your content aligns with their preferred channels, the more likely they are to engage.

But relevance doesn't end with delivery. It's important to monitor how your messages are received—and adapt. Are e-mails being opened? Are links clicked? Are there replies or follow-ups? These engagement signals tell you whether your messages are hitting the mark, and whether it's time to adjust tone, timing, or content.

Monitoring how specific individuals interact with your content gives you real-time insight into their interest—and opens a window for timely outreach to show that you are listening to your audience.

What makes content truly effective in Strategic ABM? Here are five essential practices:

- **Do your homework**: Go deep into the account's strategy, challenges, and market context to inform your messaging.
- **Address their pain points directly**: Show that you understand their specific problems—and offer relevant solutions.
- **Make it real**: Avoid generalizations. Craft messaging that reflects the account's current reality and priorities.
- **Meet them where they are**: Use the channels where the account is already active and receptive.
- **Always be adapting**: Use performance data to refine what you say, how you say it, and where you say it.

When you bring these elements together, your communication stops being noise—it becomes value. It builds credibility, earns trust, and starts the kind of dialogue that leads to real opportunities.

> "Building the right message has been critical for locking down our meeting with the VP."—Stacy Celano, Senior Client Executive, NTT Ltd

That's the power of relevant, clear, and timely communication in Strategic ABM. When you get it right, it opens doors that generic messaging never could.

Storytelling That Resonates with the Account's Specific Context

Think about your target account. Each one isn't just a logo or a name on a list; it's a living entity with a history, challenges, and aspirations. In the world of 1:1 ABM, truly connecting hinges on grasping this individual story, the unique narrative of every single account. This isn't about a broad brushstroke; it's about understanding the fine details that make them who they are. As the Strategic ABMer on the account, it's your job to shape your messages, your solutions, and how you interact in a way that genuinely speaks to their specific needs and objectives.

Doing this builds stronger ties, creates confidence, and will lead to increased revenue opportunities.

Know Their Story

Every account holds a story, waiting to be discovered. Their tale is built from their difficulties, their wins, where they stand in the market, and their main business objectives. And it's your job to understand that story. It means looking into how the business runs, what's happening in their industry, and who they compete with. By weaving information specific to the account into a compelling narrative, you can build a plot that speaks directly to their situation, using their challenges and successes as important parts of the story.

Using specific insights this way isn't just about showcasing data; it's about using data to tell a story. It means taking what you know about an account—their problems, what they've done well, their place in the market, and their objectives—and using it to create a narrative. This makes your content more relevant and interesting, and it helps set the stage for the account team to engage in discussions with key stakeholders.

The more that you do this, the more enjoyable it will become. I treat these stories like mysteries, and every time I peel back a new layer, I feel like I'm closer to figuring out who did it.

Why Your Offerings Matter

When you propose ways you can help a target account, it's crucial to explain why these ideas make sense for them. This involves showing how what you offer addresses their aims and challenges, instead of just listing what it does. By linking your solutions back to the account's own story, you show that you really understand what they need and challenge them to see that you have the best solution.

To build a sense of ease and understanding, try using language and a style that feels familiar to the account, by mirroring how they communicate internally. This helps create comfort and makes your message land better. Adopting their way of speaking shows you're aware of their community and what matters to them, which is vital for a lasting connection.

Instead of simply explaining the value you bring, it's much more powerful to show it. Use examples, run simulations, customize demonstrations, and promote on-site workshops. This gives tangible proof of how your offerings can tackle their specific problems and help them succeed. Demonstrating value in a concrete way makes a stronger impact and increases the likelihood of them wanting to engage further.

Connecting on a deeper level means pointing out shared values and common outlooks. This helps build a foundation for a long-term partnership that goes beyond a simple transaction. Showing common ground helps establish a strong basis for working together over time.

Lastly, always keep your communication brief and impactful. Respect their time by getting straight to the point and leaving a memorable impression. In the busy world of business today, being short and clear is essential for getting and keeping an account's attention. By following these ideas, you can create powerful narratives that connect with your target accounts, drive engagement, and help them find success. Understanding each account's unique story and using a tailored approach to communication lets you tap into the full power of Strategic 1:1 ABM.

Designing High-Touch Engagements

In Strategic ABM, successful engagement is built on precision. High-touch engagement means going beyond generic outreach and instead designing moments that align with the account's unique journey, stakeholders, and timing. You aren't creating just another campaign—you're creating a choreography.

It starts with a clear understanding: the sales cycle isn't a single moment. It's a sequence of decision-making milestones involving multiple stakeholders, each with their own priorities and points of influence. To design impactful experiences, you must first map their journey—not only by stage, but by role. Who's involved? When do they enter the process? What questions are they trying to answer at that point?

From there, you craft interactions that feel intentional. Each piece of content, each point of contact, each gesture of value should land at the right time, with the right message, through the right channel. This requires close collaboration with your account team to orchestrate engagement that's both relevant and well-paced. When done correctly, it creates a feeling of alignment—that you understand not just the business but the people behind the business.

That alignment is critical, especially when high-stakes opportunities are in play. One of the most important lessons here, as my father always asked, is: "What do you want me to do, *not* do, and let you do?"

Strategic ABM isn't just about bold actions—it's about intentional ones. And often, restraint is the most strategic choice you can make.

For example, there may be moments when the account enters a formal RFP process—often with strict rules about who can communicate and when. If you've done your job right, your marketing may have played a pivotal role in earning that RFP. But continuing to engage during a blackout period, even with the best intentions, can backfire. It could disqualify your team or raise concerns about compliance.

In these moments, knowing when to pause your marketing efforts—and letting the account team take the lead—is just as strategic as knowing when to act. Your role becomes one of support, not visibility.

Ultimately, designing high-touch engagements is about precision, timing, and emotional intelligence. It's knowing when to amplify, when to adapt, and when to step back. It is not just about what you say—it's about when you say it, how you say it, and most importantly, why.

Planning Account-Specific Interaction Sequences

When you're aiming to connect with key stakeholders, you quickly learn that making a sale isn't just one simple action. It's a process, a sequence of decisions and interactions. Understanding the account's buying journey is foundational to creating a relevant and engaging experience for those you hope to reach. This journey is the series of events and choices a customer makes when purchasing a product or service. Laying out this path helps you see where you can connect and influence potential customers.

To move effectively along this path, you must figure out who holds the cards. Identifying the key decision makers at each stage should have been accomplished when you were mapping your target account. That information now becomes paramount in this stage. Those key stakeholders are now your target audience.

Thinking about how you reach your target audience is the next phase of the plan. Determining optimal channels for interaction means considering the best way to communicate with someone at a given time. This is a crucial step. I've worked on Strategic ABM accounts where the key stakeholders were very decentralized. And worst of all, each key stakeholder was located in different parts of the United States, in rural towns. That meant you needed a very different tact than when you're targeting an organization like Salesforce where the majority of the senior leadership reside in the same place and operate out of the same office.

Once you've managed to understand how you plan on reaching your audience, then you can begin crafting your messaging. Crafting hyper-personalized or customized content is vital for catching the attention of key stakeholders at each step of the sales process. This means creating messages that will help lead them down the path from intent and interest to closing new opportunities. When you speak directly to their world, you are building relationships, not just trying to close today's opportunity. You need to move past the immediate win and look at the long-term potential gains.

Getting your timing right is also a key piece of this puzzle. Establishing a clear cadence and frequency for interactions balances staying connected while respecting the decision maker's schedule. It's about staying Top of Mind (ToM), not being a constant nuisance.

Finally, this isn't a one-time setup. Continuously assessing and adjusting is nonnegotiable. You need to watch how decision makers respond, look at metrics that show engagement, and refine the experience based on what you learn.

That is why leading ABM teachers and books state that Strategic ABM practitioners should not take on more than five accounts at any one time (Figure 6.1). In the article "What Is 1:1, 1:Few, and 1:Many ABM (With Real-Life Examples)," Yulia Olennikova describes how "1:1 ABM typically focuses on a smaller group of 5 to 10 high-value accounts, but it can also be focused on just one person or account."[17]

Monitoring responses and tracking how interactions are received helps ensure your approach stays relevant and effective as things progress.

[17]Olennikova (2023).

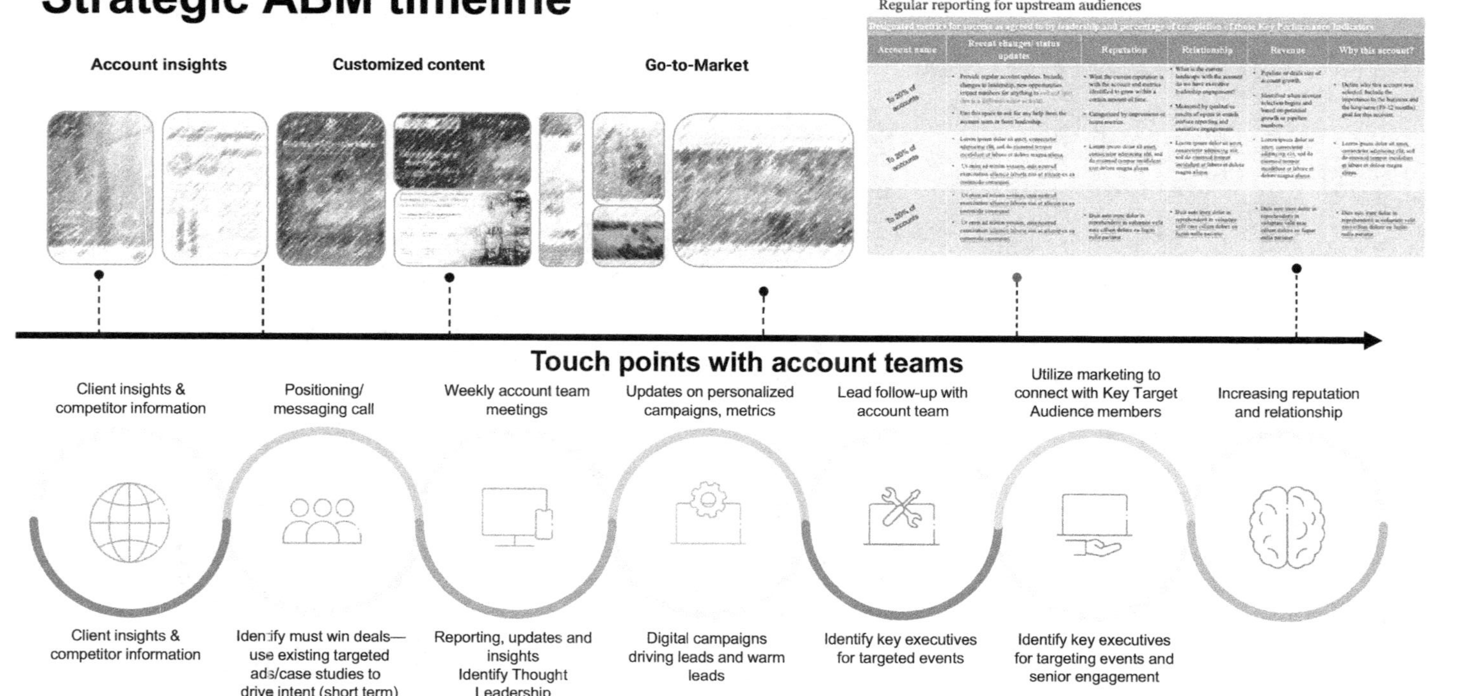

Figure 6.1 Strategic ABM timeline

These steps will help you to create an experience that speaks directly to the needs and interests of the key stakeholders who matter at each phase of their buying journey. Building trust, increasing the chance of moving the needle, and helping to drive growth and decrease the Sales Cycle Length. The Sales Cycle Length is the average time it takes for a sales team to close a deal. It should be calculated from initial contact to a closed-won sale. The formula for this is accomplished by summing the total days it takes from when opportunities are created until when they are closed-won and dividing by the number of closed-won deals. This provides key metrics both for the sales team as well as helping to showcase how ABM is affecting the overall account.

Executing Outreach Campaigns

This type of outreach focuses on people who are in leadership that are going to make an impact. Who are the champions, influencers, budget holders, and blockers? What pressures do they face? What success looks like to them may not be what's listed on a corporate website.

The stakeholder personas or empathy maps that you've created during your mapping process will help to guide your messaging. Speak their language—literally. Use the terminology, tone, and phrasing familiar to their industry, function, and business. Show them you've done more than skim a press release; prove to them that you understand their needs.

One of my favorite examples comes from an old advertising agency anecdote from the 1970s. A notoriously hard-to-please client had rejected award-winning campaigns and flooded PR coverage. Nothing worked—until one account manager sat down and spent time just talking with him. What did he learn? That the client wanted to make his mother proud. The agency bought a billboard in a small town in upstate New York—near her home—with the client's photo, job title, and accomplishments. That billboard succeeded where no campaign had. Why? Because someone finally listened.

The takeaway? You never know what truly matters to someone until you take the time to ask.

Strategic ABM success is measured less by open rates and more by *open doors*. It's about earning trust, building momentum, and being invited deeper into the conversation. Metrics matter but meaning matters more. Personalized and customized outreach that reflects real insight—about both the account and the individual—creates long-term value.

To build effective personalized outreach campaigns:

- Start with stakeholder research, not assumptions.
- Craft messaging with empathy, specificity, and intent.
- Use the appropriate channel for each contact and context.
- Align outreach with personal and professional motivations.
- Prioritize connection over automation.

When done correctly, these campaigns don't just capture attention—they create connections. And in Strategic ABM, that connection is the beginning of everything.

Executive Briefings and Bespoke Events

Connecting with the people who truly shape outcomes in business requires something beyond the everyday interaction. It demands dedicated space, a moment carved out from the relentless pace of work to sit, listen, and speak with real intent. This is where the carefully planned executive briefing or the thoughtfully designed account event comes into its own. These aren't just meetings; they are opportunities for a deep, focused exchange, allowing businesses to genuinely connect with significant figures, understand their world, and share their own vision in return.

Think of it as building a sturdy bridge, plank by plank, conversation by conversation. These moments allow your account team or executive sponsor to establish rapport, tackle specific problems they might be facing head on, and demonstrate exactly how you can contribute value, not just in theory but in a tangible, interactive way.

Getting this right starts with clarity. Before anything is scheduled or any invitation is sent, pause and ask: What do we genuinely want to achieve? Defining precise, measurable, achievable, relevant, and time-bound objectives ensures that the effort isn't a wasted motion. It means understanding the account's situation, their current needs, and their future goals. Knowing your destination allows you to plot the correct course, ensuring that the discussions held, and the information shared directly address what matters most to those involved.

With clear aims established, the next step is shaping the experience itself. The flow of the session, the topics covered—these must speak directly to the challenges and opportunities specific to that account. Simply presenting standard information won't suffice. It might involve presentations, certainly, but mixing in interactive discussions and time for informal connection can cater to how different people best absorb information and build understanding. Bringing together the right individuals from both your organization and the account creates an environment where open discussion thrives, and ideas can be shared freely.

Creating a session that feels genuinely significant means considering the environment. Where you meet and how the session unfolds should feel natural for the attendees. Thinking about their way of working, what they value—these details matter. Selecting a location and structure that aligns with their preferences signals respect and attention. This level of consideration helps create a session that isn't just informative, but feels unique and meaningful, helping to build credibility and goodwill.

What happens after the event concludes is just as vital as the event itself. The energy and insights from the discussions must translate into action. Following up effectively means reinforcing the key messages that landed, clearly outlining what happens next, and continuing to provide useful information or support. This ensures that the momentum generated isn't lost and demonstrates a continued dedication to the relationship. It keeps the conversation alive and ensures that the shared understanding leads to concrete outcomes.

Certain practices consistently lead to more impactful sessions. These include pinpointing exactly what you aim to accomplish; crafting the structure and content to fit the account's particular needs; involving the right leadership from both sides; choosing a setting that respects the account's style; and diligently following up afterward. Applying these principles, focusing on a personalized and engaging approach, can make these sessions incredibly effective instruments for building strong connections and identifying new possibilities for collaboration. Even virtual formats, structured as smaller, focused group discussions, can provide a unique opportunity for senior figures to connect and address specific concerns.

Delivering Customized Demos, Workshops, and Proposals

In Strategic ABM, every interaction should feel tailored—because if it doesn't, it risks becoming just more noise. And once you have your key stakeholder's attention, then you need to continue to go further because going back to more traditional messaging can risk losing them forever. The real power of high-touch engagement lies in delivering experiences that speak directly to the target account's unique priorities.

Take product demonstrations, for example. The traditional approach—showcasing every feature and hoping something resonates—is outdated and ineffective. In my experience, a demo is only successful if the client starts asking questions when you're presenting. It's a signal they see personal relevance.

To create that relevance, a demo must be built specifically for the account. Before you ever open your deck or launch the platform, you need to do the groundwork of knowing the account. Then it is no longer about presenting your solution—it's about showing how your solution solves *their* problem.

Real-world examples matter here. They give credibility to your claims and help prospects visualize success. When speaking to key stakeholders, time is limited. For a recent Agentic AI demo, we gave ourselves a hard cap of two minutes. That constraint forced us to focus on clarity, outcomes, and relevance—and the result landed better than any 30-slide walkthrough ever would.

Beyond demos, collaborative workshops can deepen engagement and foster buy-in. These aren't presentations—they're working sessions. Bring your team together with stakeholders from the account to cocreate potential solutions. This collaborative model not only fosters trust but also leads to solutions that reflect the account's real-world needs. Plus, it offers a side benefit: The prototype or approach developed for this account can often become a repeatable model for similar future opportunities.

When it's time to deliver a proposal, resist the urge to rely on a standard template. In Strategic ABM, proposals should feel like extensions of your understanding. They must be tailored to reflect the account's goals, business priorities, and expected outcomes. A great proposal doesn't just state what you're offering—it shows what the account will gain. It quantifies potential ROI, outlines operational impact, and connects directly to the client's broader aspirations.

But hyper-customization doesn't happen by accident—it requires process and discipline. It starts with deep research. Every conversation, every asset, and every point of outreach must align with the account's challenges and goals. Use your accumulated data and insights to guide that customization. Keep communications clear, direct, and benefit driven. This kind of intentionality turns engagement into real connection—and connection into relationships. And relationships into greater opportunities.

To assess whether your customized efforts are working, track results carefully.

- Are stakeholders engaging with personalized content?
- Are demos leading to more questions and conversations?
- Are proposal win rates increasing?
- Do workshops open doors to regular conversations with key stakeholders?

Leverage tools like Crazy Egg, Hotjar, or other heat mapping platforms to visualize how stakeholders interact with content. Utilize marketing analytics to monitor e-mail open rates, content views, and engagement with personalized microsites. Post-sale satisfaction surveys can help confirm whether expectations set during your engagement are being fulfilled.

Ultimately, putting personal relevance at the center of every interaction drives the success of Strategic ABM. It builds credibility, fosters deeper relationships, and positions your organization as a partner—not a vendor. In a world where relevance is rare, tailoring every touchpoint is your competitive advantage.

Building Account-Specific Value Propositions and Offers

Striking up a conversation with someone new often begins with a simple question: "What do you do?" In the world of marketing, particularly when focusing on target accounts, the more pertinent question is: "What do you want most to make your company successful and your job easier?" Forget the broad brushstrokes of traditional campaigns, success with specific, target accounts hinge on a deep, almost intimate understanding of their world. Call it insight gathering, reconnaissance, or just plain homework, but the effort spent here dictates everything you will do next with your Strategic ABM target accounts.

Building your foundation means truly getting inside the target account's real world. We've discussed what this means and how important it is to be inside their heads to understand their direction. Throughout college I fenced, I was even featured in an issue of American Fencing Magazine. To this day, I still tell people that I'm not a great fencer, what I am good at is getting inside my opponent's head. Being able to get inside your stakeholder's head is critical when building your 1:1 ABM campaign.

Just as crucial is sizing up the playing field around them—knowing your target accounts' key competitors, understanding where they're strong, and where they might be vulnerable. But it doesn't stop there. You should also be able to hold a mirror up to the account itself. Who makes things happen? What's their structure? Identifying the people who hold sway—the potential advocates, the influencers, the final approvers—is vital intelligence. Knowing these roles allows you to map out how decisions get made. Being able to access this information isn't easy. This is one of the reasons why I almost always refuse to take on a Strategic ABM account without knowing that there is already an existing relationship between the account team and senior decision makers.

Armed with this understanding, you can begin to speak their language. Generic sales pitches fall flat. What's needed are value propositions that feel written just for them, addressing their specific goals, easing their difficulties, and speaking to what matters most. A good way to anchor this effort is by settling on three core messaging pillars. These pillars become the guiding principles for all communication and engagement directed at that account going forward. Bringing people together and getting them to work together requires traditional leadership qualities.

This level of focus demands internal alignment. Strategic ABM is always a team effort. You must be willing to embed yourself with the account team. Collaboration between the teams who sell the solution and those who deliver it—sales, product, customer success—is nonnegotiable. Working in unison, you can construct solutions that are not only relevant but genuinely compelling. These aren't just standard packages; they're designed to feel like white-glove opportunities, explicitly demonstrating that you grasp their unique situation. The goal is to provide tangible, measurable advantages that make saying yes the clear, obvious choice.

Creating these irresistible solutions requires the insight gained from research. What precisely are their challenges? What outcomes are they chasing? By directly addressing their pain points and showing the concrete benefits your solution provides, you significantly increase the likelihood of getting their attention, growing revenue, and being considered for future opportunities.

The world doesn't stand still, and neither do account priorities or market conditions. Every day you will find new challenges when working with account teams in Strategic ABM. This is why the work isn't done once the initial plan is stood up or once the campaign first goes live. You need to constantly be hustling in the world of Strategic ABM. Regularly reviewing and refining your value propositions and offers based on ongoing monitoring of the account's evolving needs is essential. Staying nimble and agile ensures your approach remains sharp and effective.

Supporting this detailed insight gathering are various tools and technologies. Data analytics platforms can reveal patterns, CRM systems organize stakeholder information, and social listening tools that provide real-time sentiment and insights. These tools are powerful aids, but their use demands caution, especially when dealing with data outside your immediate region. Regulations like General Data Protection Regulation (GDPR) are strict, and failing to comply can lead to significant penalties and damaged trust. Ensuring data privacy isn't just a legal requirement; it's a fundamental part of building a respectful, long-term relationship with your target accounts. Prioritizing thorough research, establishing clear messaging, collaborating internally, designing compelling offers, staying adaptable, and handling data responsibly form the backbone of effective ABM.

CHAPTER 7

Implementing 1:1 ABM Operations

They realized it wasn't enough to just coexist—not when they could work together to create value for the company and for customers.
Kotler, Rackham, and Krishnaswamy 2006[18]

Aligning Sales and Marketing

Success with focused account strategies, particularly when targeting individual, high-value opportunities through 1:1 ABM, demands a united effort from Sales and Marketing. This kind of close collaboration requires a deliberate structure built on shared purpose.

There is a fundamental need for teams to commit to the same overall revenue objectives. Once confirmed then you should discuss how to establish specific revenue targets for selected target accounts and define the clear, shared ways to measure collective progress. Forecasting expected financial results with transparency ensures everyone is working from the same understanding. Achieving this level of effectiveness also depends on assigning distinct responsibilities, creating clear methods for moving accounts forward between teams, and maintaining consistent, open communication. Providing sales professionals with the specific information and resources they need further strengthens this joint approach.

This need for intentional alignment between Sales and Marketing has been outlined by Philip Kotler, Neil Rackham, and Suj Krishnaswamy in "Ending the War Between Sales and Marketing" (*Harvard Business Review*, July to August 2006). The authors emphasize that true effectiveness arises only when both sales and marketing move beyond coexistence to

[18]Philip Kotler (2006).

genuine collaboration—"working together to create value for the company and for customers." The article reinforces the notion that shared revenue objectives, transparent forecasting, and clearly defined roles are essential for achieving operational harmony and measurable growth. By linking strategic account-based initiatives to this foundational perspective, organizations can build a structured, collaborative framework that unites teams around common purpose and outcomes.

Establishing Shared Goals, KPIs, and Revenue Targets

I cannot stress enough the imperative need to be able to create alignment between Sales and Marketing in every aspect of successful Strategic ABM. You can have best-in-class strategies and highly skilled teams, but if Sales and Marketing aren't synchronized, your efforts will lack traction and you'll find yourself wasting your time and investment. As outlined in the book *Extreme Ownership* by Jocko Willink and Leif Babin, successful U.S. Navy SEAL missions rely on synchronized teamwork where everyone takes ownership and is rowing in the same direction. In ABM, that shared direction begins with clearly defined goals, unified revenue targets, and agreed-upon KPIs.

Strategic ABMers often get labeled as rule-breakers by Brand and traditional Marketing. In reality, we're just working with a different set of goals—ones that demand close alignment with Sales, flexibility in tactics, and a relentless focus on outcomes. When Sales and Marketing lock arms and agree on what success looks like, the full potential of ABM becomes unlocked. And the senior leadership will be amazed at how strong the alignment and bonds will be between these two teams.

- *Step 1: Define Revenue Targets Together*
  Before diving into execution, both teams must align on which accounts to prioritize and what revenue outcomes we aim to achieve. Think of this as choosing the most fertile ground before planting seeds. This isn't just about "big names"—it's about focusing your combined efforts on accounts with the highest potential return especially at the start.

  For example, during my time in Service Marketing, we used regional demographic data in the Puget Sound to guide our outreach. By analyzing public records—like single-family home values and growth trends in areas such as the Issaquah Highlands—we identified high-opportunity zones and tailored our outreach accordingly. This localized, data-driven strategy mirrored the precision of Strategic ABM. Rather than wasting resources on broad messaging, we zeroed in on the areas (and customers) where we could make the biggest impact. And the final step was to meet with sales to ensure that the data was accurate from a field operations point of view.

That's what defining revenue targets for each 1:1 ABM target account allows you to do—concentrate effort where it counts, based on clear, shared expectations.

- *Step 2: Align on Shared KPIs*

  Once revenue targets are in place, you need a way to track progress. That's where shared KPIs come into play. Creating shared KPIs with Sales will not only increase alignment but also increase account understanding for the ABMer.

  Your KPIs should reflect the joint priorities of both Sales and Marketing. Common KPIs in 1:1 ABM include:
  - Stakeholder engagement (e.g., number of decision makers engaged)
  - Pipeline acceleration metrics (e.g., movement from MQL to SQL [sales-qualified lead])
  - Deal velocity and size
  - Account penetration across business units
  - Increase in intent scores or personalization metrics
  - Influence on down-selected opportunities outside the current book of business

  For ABM accounts, I often include a metric tied to the number of strategic accounts onboarded per marketer. Additionally, we track how positioning pillars evolve into revenue-generating conversations and whether ABM efforts expand the account beyond its traditional footprint.

  Another powerful metric? Reduction in Sales Cycle Length. I've already spoken about how outdated processes slowed efficiency when I was at a Seattle based service company because the technicians would hand write every order. What I failed to mention was that by digitizing the process, we reclaimed 3.5 hours a day—enabling each tech to run an additional job per day per technician. That translated into $50,000 in monthly revenue growth. The same principle applies in B2B: when Marketing and Sales efforts are tightly aligned, inefficiencies fall away and performance soars.

- *Step 3: Forecast with Transparency*
  Strategic ABM isn't just about knowing your goals—it's also about predicting what's coming. Sales and Marketing must work together to create a **shared revenue forecasting model** that reflects real-time insights from both sides.

  Regular check-ins between teams help ensure forecasts stay accurate and actionable. Marketing may have insight into account engagement trends, while Sales brings updates on stakeholder dynamics or organizational shifts. Together, this gives you a full picture—and lets you spot challenges early, course-correct faster, and stay aligned around evolving targets.

  The transparency of this process also builds trust. When Marketing can show how engagement metrics correlate with pipeline movement—or how campaign influence accelerates deals—it reinforces the value of the ABM model.

Defining Roles, Responsibilities, and Hand-offs

Launching into Strategic ABM should feel like setting sail for a specific, valuable island rather than letting the wind take you where it wants. This approach, targeting select accounts with significant revenue promise, relies heavily on the Marketing and Sales teams working in unison toward that single destination. Think of it as if you are on a pirate ship out to plunder the Caribbean. For this focused journey to succeed, both teams must know exactly where they are going and who is doing what. Simply put, you need a clearly defined destination that you're navigating toward.

When roles are clear, it avoids the confusion of multiple people trying to do the same thing, or worse, nobody doing anything at all. Think of it like building something complex; each person needs their specific task.

Your job is to take charge of understanding the target accounts deeply—gathering information, finding insights. You're the one who is charting the course. It's this knowledge that allows marketing to craft messages and content that directly address those specific accounts needs and pain points.

Sales then takes these insights and runs with them, crafting custom outreach and engagement. Using the understanding provided by marketing and sales conversations to become highly relevant, speaking directly to the account's situation. This division of effort ensures focus and makes every interaction count. And that divide and conquer mentality only exists when there is trust.

Knowing that you're making progress requires a shared scorecard. Setting goals for each role, agreed upon by both Marketing and Sales, ensures everyone is sailing toward the same overall objective. When success looks the same for both teams, it naturally creates an environment of camaraderie. This shared view also makes it easier to spot what's working and where things need to be improved.

Moving an account smoothly from marketing's efforts to sales' direct engagement requires clear pathways. Establishing defined steps for when and how accounts transition between teams prevents anything from getting lost in translation. This keeps the momentum going for the target accounts, ensuring they receive consistent attention.

Underpinning all of this is regular conversation. Keeping the lines of communication open means teams stay connected, identify challenges early, and work through them quickly. This constant dialogue supports the collaborative effort and helps both sides learn from each other, making all aspects of your ABM program more effective over time. I recommend the following regular check-ins; Strategic 1:1 weekly, 1:Few monthly, 1:Many every other month.

Putting these principles into practice—clear roles, shared goals, relevant content informed by insight, consistent communication, and continuous review—helps organizations realize the full potential of all stages of ABM. It's about understanding who you're talking to and ensuring Marketing and Sales function as a single unit to deliver experiences that make a difference. With clear understanding and collaboration, the rewards of every stage of ABM become apparent.

Regular Joint Account Planning Sessions

At some point, you're going to feel like you're juggling a dozen different things at once, like everything else in today's world. You're trying to engage specific target accounts, deciding between personalized and customized messaging, manage expectations and time with account teams, trying to ensure that you do not risk damage to the current relationship, and track impact. Without a steady rhythm, it's easy for things to slip, momentum to slow, and small issues to become significant problems before you realize it.

This is where a simple, consistent cadence the account team becomes less of a bureaucratic burden and more of a lifeline. Think of it as the heartbeat of your strategic ABM efforts. Regular check-ins keep the whole operation alive and moving forward. They are where sales and marketing stop working in separate worlds and start working together toward shared goals for target accounts.

ABM is how many leaders see that marketing and sales will bridge existing gaps and come back into alignment. Misalignment between marketing and sales teams costs companies an average of 10 percent of revenue per year.[19]

Regular cadence is designed to create shared responsibility. When sales and marketing are in the room together, discussing the same accounts, looking at the same information, the ownership naturally shifts from "my job" or "their job" to "our account." And it becomes a form of building bridges across the great Sales and Marketing divide.

In case you missed it earlier, this is where a Strategic ABM leader begins to feel like being the **CMO** of their target accounts.

> "1:1 account-based marketing makes you the CMO of your accounts. It's not just about campaigns or demand—it's about owning the brand, experience, and growth strategy for every client you serve. When done right, ABM transforms marketing from a support function into a strategic driver of business value." —Matt Preschern, Global CMO, MJP Consulting

[19] O'Neill (2023).

To make these weekly meetings truly effective, each one needs structure. Walking in blind wastes everyone's time. The most productive meetings I've seen focus sharply on a few core areas. They begin with reviewing the account's objectives—what does the team and the company want us to do? Then, teams share updates on what's been happening, what initiatives are in motion, and what results are coming in. Crucially, these meetings are the place to lay bare any roadblocks or difficulties. What's stopping us? What isn't working as expected? What shouldn't the marketing and ABM team be doing? We conclude by pinpointing exactly what needs to change and assigning specific actions to specific people. What do you want us to let the account team do? This sharp focus helps teams stay on track and base their next steps on real data.

Being able to converse and be candid are paramount on getting you and the account team on the same page. It's about building an understanding of the account's situation and our collective aims. By combining insights—sales bringing the frontline perspective, marketing bringing the broader market view and campaign expertise—strategies and approaches become much stronger. Defining who is responsible for what within the account plan removes ambiguity and allows a focused effort. Before you know it, you have sales going to bat for marketing and seeing the larger picture like never before.

This process of planning together cultivates a sense of joint ownership and mutual accountability. When teams build the strategy hand-in-hand, they're both invested in its success. This kind of collaboration helps address challenges quickly and seize opportunities as they appear. We begin rowing together.

If you take nothing else from this, take the knowledge that Strategic ABM is a continuous effort. And your cadences should reflect that by including a way to learn and adapt. Setting up a feedback loop means that results from the field and from campaigns directly inform future strategy. It's how we are able to refine our methods, react to new challenges or opportunities for specific accounts, and consistently improve how they work together and the results they achieve.

Meeting regularly, with purpose and agenda items, ensures that teams remain connected and actively moving toward their account goals. It's how you stay ahead of problems, make decisions based on evidence, and continuously strengthen the partnership between sales and marketing. By putting these simple practices in place, organizations build a meeting rhythm that will push your Strategic ABM program to the next level.

Facilitating Seamless Communication and Collaboration

In 2007, I earned my motorcycle license in London and bought my first bike soon after—a moment that sparked a lifelong passion. When I think about what makes a motorcycle perform flawlessly, it always comes down to the synchronized precision between the spark plug and the piston. In a Ducati 916 engine, the piston moves rhythmically up and down, compressing air and fuel. At the exact right instant, the spark plug delivers an electric charge that ignites the mixture—creating a burst of energy that propels the motorcycle forward.

That perfect timing and coordination remind me of what's required between Sales and Marketing when building 1:1 ABM campaigns. Just as the spark plug and piston rely on one another to keep the engine running smoothly, Sales and Marketing must operate in harmony—each triggering and responding to the other's motion. When they move together with that same level of precision, targeting becomes sharper, messaging more relevant, and momentum unstoppable.

Where Alignment Begins

True collaboration starts with **clear, ongoing communication**. That means creating intentional opportunities for both sides to speak openly about account progress, share insights, and align around shared goals. This isn't just about updates; it's about building a rhythm of mutual understanding. Sara Williams, the VP of Sales for account-based go-to-market platform Demandbase, said, "poor alignment can cost businesses 10% or more of annual revenue, and 48% of enterprises still struggle with alignment." [20]

Using platforms like Slack or Microsoft Teams can facilitate quick, informal check-ins. These touchpoints help both sides stay up to date on

---

[20]Lindenau (2024).

account developments, share new intelligence, and respond rapidly to shifts in the account's needs or behaviors. And you can create questionnaires with Survey Monkey or Microsoft Forms for more formal feedback and insight.

Structure Builds Trust

Regular, structured meetings—weekly or biweekly—serve as checkpoints to track progress, troubleshoot challenges, and refine strategies in real time. These sessions should include agenda topics like:

- Current account status updates
- Key upcoming opportunities or milestones
- Feedback loops from the field
- Ask-me-anything (AMA) style inputs between teams

One of the simplest but most effective questions I've used to open these meetings is, "How can I help?" It builds trust, shows support, and invites true collaboration from day one.

And to take a page out of Amazon's internal meetings, always have an agenda. Agendas may seem boring, but they are imperative for keeping everyone on course when you're working on accounts for upward of 14 months at a time.

Create a Shared Language

A critical part of alignment is developing a shared vocabulary around Strategic ABM: success metrics, sales stages, stakeholder engagement levels, campaign types, and even content tags. When sales and marketing speak the same language, miscommunication drops and execution speeds up.

I once worked on a Strategic ABM account for over seven months, and the results spoke for themselves—literally. The CE, Carrie Walden, created a testimonial video praising the measurable impact of our collaboration. That video became a part of our internal enablement program and helped drive broader buy-in from senior leadership, and we went on an internal education program to broaden interest among sales. Alignment breeds advocacy (Figure 7.1).

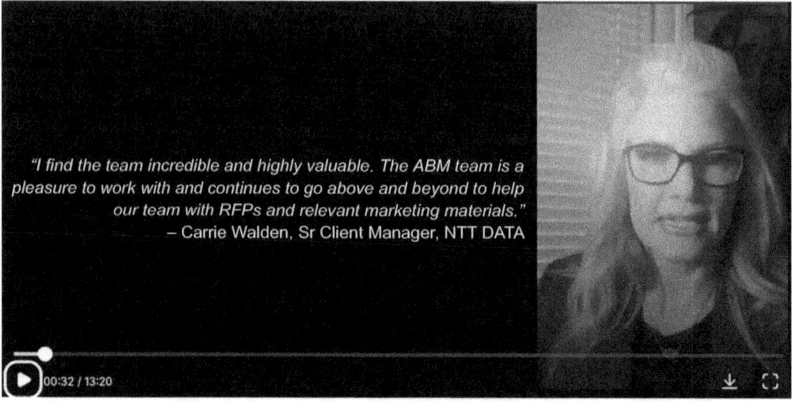

Figure 7.1 Quote from sales regarding ABM

Operational Tips to Keep in Sync

Here are some tactical moves that ensure communication and collaboration don't fall through the cracks:

- **Define shared ABM objectives** early, and revisit them often.
- **Standardize collaboration tools** and establish simple rules of use.
- **Set a cadence for joint account reviews** with clear agendas.
- **Create lightweight communication protocols** (e.g., "ping me if X happens").
- **Embed marketing in sales** to drive cross-functional visibility and develop reliance and trust.

These seemingly small practices add up to real momentum. They create the shared discipline and mutual understanding needed to win together.

Bottom Line

When sales and marketing align seamlessly, 1:1 ABM becomes more than a campaign—it becomes a partnership. With open communication, shared systems, and consistent collaboration, teams can craft more personal, relevant experiences that drive engagement, deepen relationships, and ultimately grow revenue. Strategic ABM doesn't work without this foundation—and when done right, it becomes one of your greatest competitive advantages. All of these things will help to further embed you with the account team and accelerate the processes of everyone rowing together in the same direction.

During an interview on *Let's talk ABM*, I was asked a deceptively simple question: "What has been your greatest learning?"

For me, it comes down to a genuine eagerness—to wake up each day excited to connect with peers and account teams, and to collectively explore new ways to move an account forward. It's the energy that comes from true partnership with Sales, where ideas flow freely, perspectives are valued, and listening goes both ways.

When trust exists, collaboration stops feeling transactional and is done with true purpose. It's in those moments—working side by side, aligned around shared goals—that we create campaigns that are not just well executed but deeply relevant and truly impactful for our most important accounts.

Enabling Sales with Account Insights, Content, and Tools

Often, in ABM there's a disconnect between the sophisticated targeting done by marketing and the reality faced by sales teams tasked with talking to these accounts. Without the right gear, even the best-laid ABM plans will stumble.

Think of it like sending someone into a complex negotiation without any briefing materials or even a notepad. For Strategic ABM to hit its mark, you have to make sure the target account has exactly what they need, right when they need it. It's about giving them the ability to create a better reputation for the company; develop deeper relationships with their target accounts, building trust; and, eventually, grow the business revenue. Reputation, Relationship, and Revenue. We always come back to the three R's of ABM.

A corner piece of this puzzle is making sure sales has the tools and insight specific to the accounts they're pursuing. Not just generic services and products sheets, but content like case studies that mirror the account's industry challenges, whitepapers addressing their known pain points, or webinars relevant to their business goals. When the account team has this kind of tailored material at their fingertips, they can spend less time searching and more time focusing on understanding and challenging the account and offering value.

Where does all the information live? Scattered data is useless data. It's critical to pull all account knowledge into one place. Imagine a single spot where a sales rep can see contact details, company structure, and every past interaction the company has had with that account. This central platform or repository becomes the trusted source, providing the context needed to grasp the account's history and current situation quickly.

But having the tools and data isn't enough if no one knows how to use them. Investing in training is a constant. Account teams need to feel comfortable digging into the data, figuring out how to personalize messages based on what they find, and using content effectively in their outreach. Equipping them with these skills makes them more confident and significantly boosts the potential of your ABM approach. I schedule about an hour a month during the first four to six months after an account "Goes Live," for ongoing training, making sure they are using the tools and information that the ABM program can provide.

Part of that dedicated support means providing content specifically crafted for account needs. A part that isn't always discussed is the customized content that is created and curated for the account teams. You will have multiple internal audiences that you need to be aware of when developing customized collateral.

ABM will always have multiple audiences. Because of this you need to always be considering them in the back of your mind when working on a Strategic ABM account. Example: Will the Senior Leadership and Brand approve this new content that we are creating? How does your content benefit the target account? Will the account team be able to use the personalized content and how will it impact the client relationship? What pressure does this put on the larger marketing team, and will they be able to possibly lift and shift this process downstream?

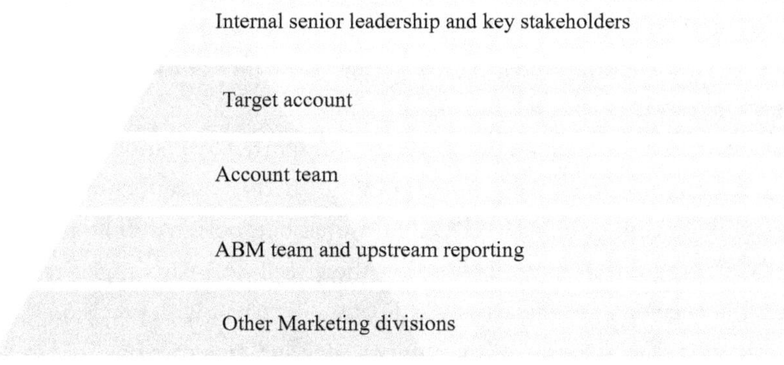

Figure 7.2 Maslow's hierarchy of strategic ABM needs

This is where frameworks like **Maslow's Hierarchy of Strategic ABM Needs** can be unexpectedly useful (Figure 7.2). If you understand where your audience operates on the pyramid—whether they're focused on stability, growth, esteem, or transformation—you can tailor your message to meet them there. This is another place where personal relevance shows that it isn't just about the company's goals; it's also about the person's goals.

When we properly equip the account team with the necessary tools and resources—the right content, a unified data source, training, and personalized content—they can move beyond generic outreach. They can concentrate on building better relationships, providing real thought leadership and value, and ultimately helping move those target accounts revenue. This focus on empowering sales is how you really amplify the effort put into your ABM program.

Leveraging Technology and Tools

Succeeding in Strategic ABM means focusing on particular demands on the systems and tools you have implemented. Unlike methods aimed at large groups, effective ABM requires a distinct technical foundation. Building a successful campaign depends on having the right set of technologies designed for this purpose.

Your CRM that holds all the details about target accounts, serving as the central point for account information is the heart of your work. Upon this base, tools for automating marketing allow for crafting and sending personalized messages to individuals within those accounts. Delivering content specific to each account's needs is supported by platforms managing tailored resources. And understanding whether these focused efforts are working comes from specialized measurement tools that show account activity, progress, and results. Putting these technical parts together creates the necessary structure to execute Strategic ABM with precision.

In today's world we have the ability to develop hyperpersonalized messaging that account teams can further customize, then automate through marketing platforms like Eloqua by Oracle or Pardot by Salesforce to ensure the moments when target audiences are looking to engage. You can identify that intent with the help of ABM tools like Demandbase, 6sense, or DemandScience (formally Terminus), or other B2B Go-to-Market advertising automation tools that can plug into your CRM platform. By identifying intent spikes in buyer's interest, you can trigger timely messages from CEs—delivered during those intent-rich windows and sent from a real person, not a generic company alias.

When your CRM and marketing automation systems are properly synced, it's critical that account team members keep contact records up-to-date. Only then can those contacts be eligible for e-mail outreach. This alignment also enables real-time ABM reporting, giving you clear visibility into campaign performance and next-step opportunities.

Identifying the Core ABM Technology Stack for 1:1

Think about the difference between getting a generic flyer in the mail and receiving a letter that speaks directly to something you care about, mentioning you by name and perhaps referencing a challenge you've recently faced. That tailored message feels different, doesn't it? Now you're creating a real connection, this should be your whole purpose for creating your Strategic ABM program.

Achieving that level of customization, especially at scale, isn't simple. It asks for a specific way of thinking about technology—one that supports highly focused, targeted efforts. At the heart of a successful Strategic

ABM program sits a technology stack or martech stack, chosen carefully to meet those particular needs. Think of it as building a specialized toolkit designed for precision work, not mass production.

Every solid structure needs a foundation, and for Strategic ABM, that's your CRM system. It's where all the details about your target accounts live—who they are, their history with your business, the people who work there, their previous purchases and interactions. Having this information gathered in one spot gives you a clear picture of each account. This clarity helps businesses truly understand the specifics of those they want to reach, including the key people who make decisions, the problems they're trying to solve, and how they've interacted with you before.

Built upon your foundational data is your marketing automation platform. It will allow you to actually run personal campaigns. These systems make it possible to send messages targeted not just at a company but at individuals within it. This capability allows businesses to shape their marketing actions specifically for certain accounts and their decision makers. By automating repetitive tasks and setting up workflows, marketing automation also helps reduce the difficulty and manageability challenges that can come with focusing on accounts one by one. Not to mention creating conditional logic rules or IFTTT automation. Allowing for your responses or actions to be automated without any prompts from you or your team. Increasing the likelihood of passing on a potential warm lead instead of just an initial touchpoint to the account team.

Delivering the right information to the right person at the right time is essential. Content management systems (CMS) are key for holding and distributing content assets made specifically for individual accounts. By providing resources made to address the specific issues each account faces, businesses can position themselves as thought leaders in their field. A CMS that works well with other systems also helps share content smoothly across different ways of communicating, making sure target accounts get information that is relevant and arrives when they need it.

Showing that your efforts are making a difference is a cornerstone of ABM. This is where ABM platforms become important. They provide essential analysis and insights for measuring how effective 1:1 ABM campaigns are. By tracking how accounts engage, their progress, and ultimately, the ROI from these personalized actions, organizations can improve their methods and refine their technology choices for better outcomes. ABM platforms also help spot areas that need improvement. And there are pros and cons for each major platform out there today. Demandbase allows for a personalization of multiple web pages. This allows you to customize pages like the homepage and put personalized messages and relevant content that speaks directly to a target account. DemandScience offers page interrupts and Exit Intent visitor engagement. Interrupts allow for pop-ups to occur on specified pages or sections of your site, while Exit Intent creates a form fill or other engagement message when a user begins to navigate away from a page. This allows for the elimination of gated content and increased quality of leads by capturing potential leads on the way off the page. All of these are based on your system being able to identify your audience and connect them to a specific account in your CRM. Which is why it's always important to conduct regular audits of your CRM. Whichever ABM platform you choose, you need to spend time to really understand your goals that you wish to accomplish.

For all these components to work together effectively, they need to connect smoothly. A successful 1:1 ABM marketing technology stack requires the different pieces to integrate seamlessly. When CRM, marketing automation, content management, and ABM platforms work together, businesses create a coordinated and effective way of executing 1:1 ABM campaigns. This connection allows information and insights to move freely, ensuring that each part of the technology setup is used to its fullest potential.

When you're identifying and developing your 1:1 ABM martech stack, there are some key steps to keep in mind (Figure 7.3). It's smart to start by defining clear aims for your program, such as which accounts you'll target, how you'll measure engagement, and what ROI to expect. Look closely at the technology and infrastructure you already have to help find what's missing or could be better. Make sure to pick technology that connects easily with other systems, so everything works together without friction. Plan out what content you'll create to address the particular problems and needs of your target accounts. Finally, continuously watch and improve your 1:1 ABM martech stack,

Martech Landscape

Layer	Tools
Account Strategy & Planning Developing strategies and insights into a shared, actionable account plan.	Microsoft PowerPoint Miro Lucid Confluence Notion
Account Intelligence & Insight (Listening Layer) Systematically identify and prioritize each strategic account focused planning and engagement.	Demandbase 6sense Terminus Bombora LinkedIn Sales Navigator Sprout Social
Foundational CRM Layer The single source of truth that anchors every 1:1 ABM motion.	Salesforces Oracle CX Sales Hubspot CRM Microsoft Dynamics 365 SAP Sales Cloud Zoho CRM
Orchestration & Activation Coordinates and activates seamless, 1:1 engagement across sales and marketing.	Salesloft Marketo Hubspot Marketing Hub Outreach Pardot Oracle Eloqua
Bespoke Engagement Delivering personalized and customized account experiences informed by CRM context.	Canva Uberflip Vidyard PathFactory VMG Studios HALO Branded Solutions
Stakeholder Relationships Strengthen human connections with individuals and building lasting relationships.	LinkedIn Sendoso Reachdesk Hootsuite Sprout Social People.ai Pardot Oracle Eloqua Oktopost
Measurement, Revenue & Optimization Reporting platforms that prove impact, influence revenue, and refine strategy.	PowerBI Demandbase Salesforce Reports Hubspot CRM Oracle CSX Sales Google Analytics Adobe Target Optimizely Moz

Figure 7.3 Martech landscape

using the information and insights you gather to guide your decisions and keep improving. Following these essential steps and using a carefully chosen technology setup can help you achieve the full capabilities of Strategic ABM and drive long-term relationship growth and ultimately increase of revenue from target accounts.[21]

Utilizing **CRM** *as the Central Source of Account Intelligence*

Every tool that you bring into your program needs a solid foundation, your Strategic ABM program rests squarely on a robust CRM system. Think of the CRM not just as a contact list but the very engine that drives this targeted approach. I know that I've said it before, but I can't relate to you the number of times I've had headaches because the CRM isn't updated or properly maintained. One of the key things that you're CRM can do to help automate any potential issues is that you can add a standard 1:1 ABM button to accounts. When ticked on it flags that this is a target account to be removed from all other marketing activities. Which is much easier than going to each department and opting out of messaging that can cause conflicting issues as you proceed.

Successful 1:1 ABM campaigns, always need a single source of truth for every account. Bringing all account data together within the CRM is step one. This isn't just names and addresses; it's who the contacts are, what conversations you've had, the entire history of the relationship. Every medium-scale to large-scale company needs to have a CRM in place in today's world. And every marketer should be learning the ins and outs of your chosen platform.

Once the data is centralized, you can truly see how an account is engaging across marketing, sales, and service. Tracking these interactions provides a unified view. This visibility lets teams coordinate and customize their approach for each account. Using the data collected helps identify the key decision makers. Knowing who they are allows you to begin building bespoke strategies that will develop relationships.

As previously stated, Strategic ABM is not meant for prospects; you should be selecting accounts that you already have relevant data to pull

[21]Mela (2021).

from in your CRM. This allows you to look closely at your target account to craft messages and collateral that speak directly to their needs and interests. This level of customization will be important in building trust and connecting with your target audience at a deeper level, which drives revenue and decreases the time of the sales cycle.

Bringing marketing automation into focus, connected to your CRM, means you can execute targeted campaigns powered by those specific insights. This link automates repetitive tasks, freeing up your team to focus on strategy rather than manual work. Combining the rich data from the CRM with automation creates highly focused campaigns designed to get attention and convert interest and intent into action.

Constantly reviewing the data within the CRM is essential for understanding if your efforts are effective. Tagging opportunities with campaign codes allows you to track metrics like how often accounts engage, how many convert, and the revenue generated allows you to see how effective you are. In some cases, I've seen that ABM could be reporting up to one-third of marketing influenced pipeline revenue during a fiscal year. This analysis isn't just about reporting; it's about refining your strategies and making campaigns better based on real results.

Remember, the data itself needs constant attention. Keeping the CRM accurate and relevant requires regular updates with new information and market intelligence. This means ongoing efforts to add details, verify what you have, and clean-up anything outdated. Keeping the data current ensures the CRM remains a reliable foundation for making sound decisions and constantly improving your ABM program.

Building this strong CRM foundation—centralizing data, tracking engagement, customizing outreach, integrating automation, analyzing results, and maintaining data quality—provides the structure needed for successful 1:1 ABM operations. It's the practical groundwork for growing revenue and achieving lasting success with targeted marketing.

Personalization of Platforms and Tools for Execution

Try having a truly meaningful conversation with your pet. That's what trying to execute Strategic ABM feels like without the right tools. As the pet owner, you may think that your pet really understands you, but they are probably just waiting for you to give them a treat or rub their belly. Being able to reach target accounts, and the individuals within them, isn't about talking at key stakeholders; it's about connection and creating a conversation with them. While talking at people can work, that tends to be more a lead generation and brand development tool that you would execute at the top of the sales funnel. Always remember that Strategic ABM should be executed down funnel.

Choosing the right platform for your ABM program takes more than a quick comparison—it requires strategic consideration. The complexity of your ABM efforts and how well any new tool integrates with your existing martech stack are critical factors. Seamless integration is essential. You want systems that talk to each other, not silos that stall your workflow.

For larger organizations, this is where a **Center of Excellence (CoE)** becomes a real asset. A well-run CoE ensures that tools are properly integrated and operational, freeing Strategic ABMers from the burden of being the sole orchestrator. If you've ever managed even five 1:1 ABM accounts, you know—your time gets consumed fast.

Clear roles and defined responsibilities across the team aren't just helpful—they're vital to success. "One of the most important things that an ABM manager can do is create clarity with their account. Making sure that they understand that there is an ask of them creates the necessary alignment to bring everyone onto the same page," said Rachael Bell, VP of Account-Based Marketing at NTT DATA. Over the past four years, I've had the privilege of working closely with Rachael, whose leadership and vision have consistently inspired alignment and collaboration. Her deep understanding of how to build and run a CoE has taught me a great deal about how you should structure teams, delegate effectively, and align everyone to the shared goal of creating meaningful impact through Strategic ABM. We are usually referred to as ABM purists by our peers.

When deciding which platforms to choose for your martech stack, take a hard look at what the platform can do with the personalized and customized content you want to create. Does it handle different types, supporting video, web experiences, e-mail, and more? Can it grow with you? ABM programs are always the most flexible, I usually tell people that ABM is like working for an agency but in-house. And that means you need to pick a platform that's built to scale and offers the flexibility you need.

Beyond just delivery, effective tools provide ways to track what target audiences are actually doing with your customized content. You can monitor usage and measure if your efforts are on target. Your martech stack should give you data that you can act on—insights that show what's working and where you need to tweak your approach to improve results continuously.

Putting these platforms to work effectively isn't just flipping a switch. There are steps that make a big difference. One is building out a solid content foundation. Think of it as a modular system: base messaging that can be adapted, presentation decks you can edit for a specific account, case studies relevant to a particular industry, thought leadership pieces, and adaptable e-mail sequences or call scripts.

Define your metrics for success and how you'll measure it. Set clear objectives and the metrics you'll use to judge success. And finally, keep looking at the performance data. With Strategic ABM you will never just set it and forget it. Regularly review how your content is performing and adjust your strategies to make sure you're delivering the most effective message possible and maximizing engagement. Getting the platform choice right and putting it into practice following these ideas helps businesses deliver content experiences that truly connect, driving engagement, moving accounts toward conversion, and contributing to the third R in ABM, **Revenue**.

Measurement and Analytics Tools for Tracking Progress

Measuring the real impact of marketing aimed at a select few accounts requires a different kind of lens. Think about standard marketing measurements—clicks, impressions, leads generated. They tell you if and how you are reaching your audience. But when you're focused on one or a handful of specific audiences, that picture isn't sharp enough. It's like trying to assess a personal conversation by counting how many people walked past a booth.

To genuinely understand if you're making headway with those chosen accounts, you need specialized ways to look at things. This is where tools built for ABM work come into their own. They provide the detailed view you need to see what's working and what isn't when you're talking directly to key contacts within a company.

One foundational element for getting these deep insights is tying your marketing efforts directly into where you manage customer details. Connecting your marketing activity tracking with your CRM system brings all that information together. It lets you see, in one place, every interaction an account has had—whether they opened an e-mail, visited a specific page, or downloaded a piece of content. This combined perspective paints a much clearer picture of an account's interest and activity.

Platforms designed specifically for account-based strategies take this further. They offer views and reports focused squarely on your target accounts. Instead of general performance dashboards, you get to see how specific companies are engaging. Are they clicking e-mails? Are they viewing important documents? Are audiences within the account interacting with your social media? These platforms provide a direct line of sight into that account-level behavior.

And it's not just about what happens online. Understanding account activity means tracking engagement across every touchpoint. Did someone from the account attend an event? Did they also respond to a thought leadership e-mail or newsletter? Pulling together data from digital spaces and offline interactions gives you the full scope of how a target account is connecting with your message and team.

When you look at the data for these specific accounts, certain measures become particularly telling. An account engagement score rolls up all those interactions into one number, giving you a quick sense of when to reach out. Watching conversion rates between stages of the sales process for target accounts shows if your efforts are helping them move forward. Deal Velocity, or how quickly a deal progresses, often speeds up when ABM is effective. And ultimately, successful ABM can contribute to the long-term value an account brings, impacting CLV.

Gathering all the relevant account data isn't just for looking back; it's about looking forward. Using insights from your integrated CRM data, ABM platform reports, and multichannel tracking lets you see what resonates and what falls flat. This knowledge helps you fine-tune your approach for each account, making sure your messages are on point and ultimately getting better results from your account-focused efforts.

Integrating the Martech Stack for a Unified View

Let's return to your **ISAP**. You're assembling insights on key individuals across the account—but their data lives in disconnected systems. You might have contact information in one platform, engagement history in another, and stray notes sitting in someone's inbox. Without integration, it's fragmented chaos.

That's why a unified martech stack becomes essential. By integrating your systems—anchored by your CRM—you create a centralized hub where all account data comes together in one place. This integrated view ensures every team member sees the same, up-to-date narrative about the account. It allows for consistent, coordinated engagement across all channels. And it's why understanding your technology stack is fundamental to executing Strategic ABM effectively—and sustaining long-term results.

Once that integrated foundation is in place, **marketing automation** helps bring your ISAP to life. Using behavioral and firmographic insights, automation tools enable you to deliver tailored messages—sending the right content, to the right person, at exactly the right time. Instead of a mass message, it feels like a personal conversation—and that shift dramatically increases your chance of engagement.

Next comes focus. **Sales intelligence tools** sharpen your understanding of the account's structure. They help identify the right contacts, map the org chart, and reveal who influences decisions, who signs off, and who might block progress. With this intelligence, you can create engagement strategies that speak to the specific needs and roles of each stakeholder.

But how do you know if it's working? That's where **measurement and analytics** come in. Tracking key metrics—like engagement rates, conversion rates, deal velocity, and revenue impact—lets you assess what's working and what's not. This combined with regular meetings with the account team creates a feedback loop that is critical for refining both your martech stack and even influencing your broader ABM strategy.

When you connect your **CRM**, **marketing automation**, **sales intelligence**, and **analytics platforms**, you build a high-performing, unified martech stack that allows you to:

- Gain a full-picture view of each strategic account.
- Deliver personalized experiences at scale.
- Identify key players with precision.
- Optimize and improve through measurable insights.

In the Real World

Achieving seamless martech integration requires discipline and consistency. It begins with maintaining high-quality data across every system and establishing clear protocols for how that data is captured, integrated, and maintained. As Jim Fowler notes, business intelligence may be projected to grow into a $26.9 billion industry, but its solutions are only as good as the data behind them. Data integrity isn't just a technical requirement—it's the foundation that determines whether your personalization, targeting, and measurement efforts succeed or fail.

Equally important is ensuring your team understands not just how to use the tools but how to apply them strategically within a 1:1 ABM context. Fowler describes how poor data discipline creates what he calls a "rat's nest"—dirty, duplicate, or dead information that obscures insight and confuses decision making. In ABM, that kind of data chaos can undermine even the most well-built martech stack, resulting in fragmented account views and misaligned engagement strategies.

To avoid that, ABM leaders must adopt what Fowler calls a **data backbone** approach—anchoring all records around a single, globally recognized identifier. In practice, that means connecting CRM, enterprise resource planning (ERP), and ABM systems through unified fields (e.g., a company URL or unique account ID) to ensure every touchpoint references the same account reality. Clean, connected data forms the bridge that allows marketing, sales, and operations to communicate seamlessly, turning information into intelligence and intelligence into coordinated action.

Regular audits and refinements of your martech stack are essential to keep performance at its peak. Inevitably, challenges will emerge—whether from legacy systems, siloed platforms, or data accuracy issues—but confronting them directly turns those challenges into opportunities to strengthen your ABM foundation.

> *"Clean data construction is the way forward, and to ignore the need is to sacrifice your competitive edge."—Fowler, Jim, "You Can Make Your Sales Data a Lot Better with a Little Discipline," Harvard Business Review*[22]

In my own experience, I've leveraged our martech stack to surface buying intent and engagement signals using tools like Sales Navigator and a go-to-market insights platform integrated with our CRM. This enabled me to identify key decision makers based on LinkedIn activity, verify their contact information through a B2B intelligence platform, and equip our account teams with tailored case studies and targeted nurture e-mails aligned to that audience's specific challenges. These quick-turn, high-precision campaigns often act as a real-time audit of tool accuracy and alignment—what one colleague called "striking while the iron is hot."

Ultimately, integration isn't about technology for its own sake—it's about building connected intelligence and operational clarity that make every engagement more relevant, timely, and effective.

[22]Fowler (2017).

CHAPTER 8

Real-Life Success Stories and Lessons Learned

Effective Experiences of 1:1 ABM

From increasing contract value in complex software sales, to strengthening relationships through tailored solutions in B2B environments, Strategic ABM is making a measurable impact. It's driving repeat purchases and higher CLV for luxury brands, while also increasing service adoption through precise, targeted messaging—especially across Europe and North America. This is based on findings from Industryorg.com's published report, "ABM Market Set to Reach $3.9 billion by 2030, Fueled by Rising Adoption of Hyper-Personalized Marketing Strategies," that shows a compound annual growth rate (CAGR) of 14.9 percent for ABM.[23]

If your goal is to build a stronger reputation with key accounts, deepen connections with senior decision makers, and grow revenue from those relationships, Strategic ABM isn't just an option—it's the most effective marketing approach to get you there. And with 99 percent of marketers reporting higher ROI while using ABM strategies, ABM is becoming a necessity in today's world.[24]

Achieving your desired ABM outcomes will require a deep grasp of individual account circumstances and market particulars. It demands significantly on the ability to be able to address different situations and local specificities effectively. The success seen in varied environments provides important learnings, showing the value of customized methods and offering useful insights for future initiatives.

---

[23]IndustryARC (2024).
[24]Conklin (2024).

Successfully standing up 1:1 ABM campaigns involve setting clear, measurable aims from the start, understanding the specific challenges faced by the target account, and ensuring information reaches the correct individuals at the appropriate moment in their path. Customization goes deeper than using names; it means truly understanding needs to drive engagement. Success is measured not only by revenue but also by the strength of connections, advocacy, and strategic fit. Providing a highly personalized experience, including customized content and executive briefings with specific insights, is crucial for building strong connections and driving quantifiable outcomes like increased deal size and speed to close. Tracking important metrics and showing the return on this focused investment is essential for continued success.

These examples and strategies highlight the potential of 1:1 ABM campaigns to drive tangible results across diverse sectors and geographies. By understanding the unique needs and challenges of each account, businesses can develop targeted approaches that resonate with their target audience and drive long-term growth.

Illustrative Examples from My Diverse Background

When I think about how businesses truly connect with the people who matter most, it always comes back to one essential principle: know your audience. This isn't a new idea. Tailoring messaging to key clients dates back to the 1920s with pioneers like Marcel Bleustein-Blanchet. Still, it wasn't until 2003 that Bev Burgess and ITSMA gave it a formal name: Account-Based Marketing or ABM. Since then, ABM has evolved into a strategic mindset—one that unites marketing, sales, and delivery teams around shared outcomes, fluid communication, and relationship-building with high-value individuals.

At its most effective, ABM is deeply personal. The 1:1 campaign approach—focused on account-specific engagement—continues to prove its value across industries and markets. Whether in complex B2B software sales or fast-moving consumer sectors, personalized strategies lead to greater deal sizes, higher retention, and stronger cross-sell and upsell opportunities.

I've seen this firsthand across both Europe and North America. For example, in high-end consumer goods, targeting individual buyers with personalized content led not only to increased frequency of purchases, but also to significant growth in CLV. In a B2C service environment, tailoring messaging to speak directly to individual behaviors and pain points improved velocity and drove more frequent use of the service.

One particularly memorable experience came during my time at KRISPIN Marketing, where I managed the European Commission's booth at the Deutsche Messe in Hannover, Germany in 2009. The companies within the delegation weren't looking for traditional trade show setups—they valued connection over collateral. After listening closely to their needs, we designed a semiprivate lounge space that prioritized relationship-building over sales materials. We brought in local students from the Leibniz University of Hannover as servers, offered drinks and small bites, and allowed participating companies to reserve the space for informal meetings.

The result? A warm, approachable environment where stakeholders could network, share ideas, and form European and beyond partnerships—creating a sense of personal connection that impressed senior decision makers.

This story reinforces a universal truth in ABM: Flexibility and local sensitivity matter. Success depends on understanding not just what to say but *how* to say it—shaped by cultural nuance, regional behavior, and communication style. Whether you're engaging C-level executives in London or niche service providers in Seattle, relevance and resonance come from knowing exactly who you're talking to and shaping everything around *them*.

Analyzing Successful 1:1 Campaigns and Initiatives

Learning from mistakes is a common refrain, a piece of wisdom passed down in many fields. Yet, sometimes, the most powerful lessons come not from failure, but from dissecting success. What worked? Why did it work? Applying this idea to ABM, particularly the focused world of

Strategic ABM, offers a wealth of insight. Looking closely at campaigns that are on target provides valuable knowledge that can sharpen future efforts, refine methods, and enhance the overall approach to engaging specific, high-value accounts.

For 1:1 ABM campaigns to land effectively, establishing clear, quantifiable aims from the start is a fundamental step. This means pinpointing precise targets, whether that involves increasing interaction, driving desired actions, or boosting revenue numbers. Knowing what success looks like upfront enables the shaping of campaigns specifically to meet those aims and track progress along the way.

Having a deep understanding of the issues facing a target account's business is also critical for crafting customized responses and messages that truly speak to them. This requires diligent investigation into the account's industry, their company structure, and the specific difficulties they face. By grasping their challenges, you will create focused content and campaigns that connect with a target audience and offer genuine insight and thought leadership.

The Value of Thought Leadership 2025 report from Momentum ITSMA shows that 68 percent of B2B executives have increased regular consumption of thought leadership marketing content. And 99 percent of senior leadership see thought leadership as crucial when evaluating potential advisers. Matching content to the prospect's progress within the account is similarly necessary. This ensures that the right information reaches the right individuals precisely when they should be engaging with it. It involves developing content that addresses the requirements and concerns of each person involved, from first becoming aware of a need through evaluating options to making a choice. Shaping clearly defined content to fit the buyer's path helps increase engagement, build confidence, and drive relationships.

Making interactions personal will be paramount to a successful 1:1 ABM campaign. Understanding individual needs and what they prefer drives interaction and builds confidence. This is where Ethos from the rhetorical triangle from persuasive communication comes into play (Figure 8.1).

Ethos refers to the credibility and character of the speaker or writer in the rhetorical triangle. It establishes trust by demonstrating authority,

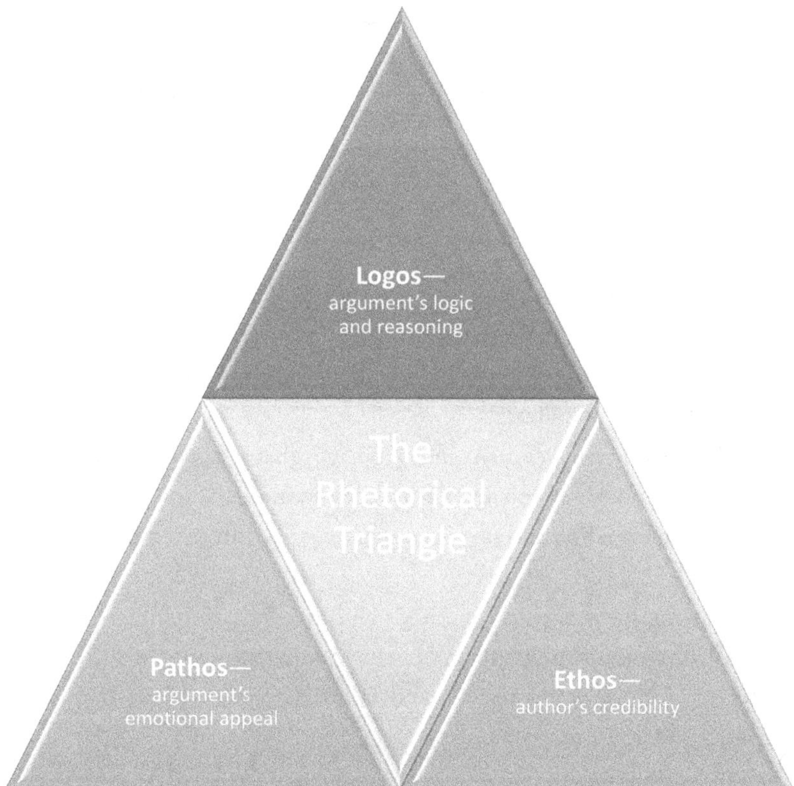

Figure 8.1 The rhetorical triangle

expertise, and shared values with the audience. Your target audience will not take notice of what you're saying to them just because they know the Client Executive's (CE) name. They will take notice because the content you're sending them is relevant to their needs and address their pain points. And once they begin to take notice then they will begin to trust you, Ethos.

> "The play's the thing wherein I'll catch the conscience of the king."
> —Hamlet, Shakespeare[25]

Checking and adjusting your strategy regularly is also necessary to ensure your efforts are having the greatest effect. This means monitoring the

[25]Shakespeare (1992).

numbers, such as how people are engaging, how many are taking desired actions, and what growth you are seeing. Using hard facts to refine the campaign strategy allows for better results, a stronger ROI, and achieving success over time.

To gain the most from examining campaigns that succeeded, ABMers should:

- Identify the main measurements and benchmarks for what counts as successful.
- Conduct thorough investigation into the target account's business difficulties and aims.
- Develop focused content and campaigns that speak to the audience.
- Continuously check and adjust the method to improve results.
- Use information and understanding to guide future campaign plans.

Following these effective methods and incorporating understandings gained from successful campaigns helps marketers improve their ABM strategies, achieve better results, and build success that lasts both with accounts and account teams.

Key Takeaways from Different Industry and Account Scenarios

It is always important to understand how important it is for people to be seen, truly seen. Not just as one face in a crowd, but as an individual with unique concerns and hopes. When you take the time to understand someone specifically, your interaction changes. It becomes more meaningful, and you are more likely to make a real connection with your target audience. This basic observation holds a powerful truth for how businesses connect with other businesses, especially when focusing on a select group of important clients.

I used to tell people that I didn't bother learning people's names, I would just classify you as Steve or Bob. Steves were people that I wanted to talk to again and Bobs were not. Because when I did learn someone's name it created this idea that I cared even more about them because I took the time to learn their name. This was totally not true; I'm just not great at remembering people's names. But I still use this type of trick when I'm teaching fencing to young people. I pretend to not learn their names at first and when I do, they feel like they've won my respect and pay more attention when I speak.

In focusing efforts on target accounts, making things personal is the point. It's about shaping your approach to fit the exact requirements and preferences of those specific target companies. When you shape what you do to meet their unique circumstances, you build a more compelling and useful interaction. This way of working helps win over new clients and strengthen bonds with existing ones, and yes, it moves the needle for the business.

Getting to Know Them: The Basis for Being Truly Personal

Getting a deep sense of what a company needs forms the bedrock for being truly personal. This involves gathering and examining information about the target company's field, how they operate internally, the problems they face, and what they hope to achieve. By doing this, you can craft messages and proposals that truly connect with the company's specific challenges and aspirations. When I created marketing for a local Seattle HVAC company, I would ride along with the guys once every other month. It would cost me a day of messaging but provide massive insights to what they were facing in real time and what customers truly cared about. In the world of B2B, I achieve this by asking to be included in quarterly business reviews (QBRs) and even client meetings to showcase messaging that we've created, ensuring it resonates with those clients that we have an existing relationship with. By following this path and creating experiences that feel made just for a target account, we are able to achieve better results in finding new clients, building stronger connections, and growing the business.

Shared Ideas, Different Worlds

While the specific ways things are done might differ across various fields, the central ideas for focusing on key companies stay consistent. The focus on individual interaction, approaches centered on the company itself, and working in tune with what the customer needs are common across the board. Whether in technology, health care, or finance, you can adapt these concepts to help things move forward and increase engagement.

Leadership Matters: Getting Support from the Top

Having leaders on board is critical for Strategic ABM to succeed. When those at the top support the strategies, it ensures the necessary resources and influence are available, helping things move forward and increasing engagement. By working toward what the leaders want to achieve, those leading the marketing efforts can show the value of this approach in reaching business objectives. This cooperation also helps different teams work together better, like marketing and sales, further improving how well these strategies work. More importantly, when getting any type of ABM initially stood up, it will take time. Time for account teams to trust you. Time for senior executives to see real and lasting results. Having that support from the top will play a key role in adoption and longevity.

Remember to Stretch and Stay Agile: Adapting as Change Happens

An account's needs will change over time. That is why being able to adjust your approach is vital when executing 1:1 ABM campaigns. You must be ready to change your strategies to reflect new needs at the account level, shifts in the industry, and market conditions. This means watching closely what the company is doing, listening for feedback, and reading annual reports and social media posts. And it means you need to be ready to shift your approach at the drop of a hat. By being agile, you can ensure your efforts remain relevant and make an impact.

Success Is More Than Just the Numbers

While revenue growth is a tangible marker of success, it only tells part of the story. True achievement in Strategic ABM is measured by the depth and durability of the relationships you build. How strong is the trust between your teams and the client's leadership? Do they advocate for your brand when you're not in the room? Have you demonstrated strategic alignment that proves your partnership goes beyond transactions to transformation?

These questions reveal the real heartbeat of ABM—the quality of engagement, the strength of collaboration, and the mutual belief that your success is intertwined.

I managed a Strategic ABM account for a global technology company specializing in transportation systems and solutions for nearly a year. Through focused, 1:1 engagement and a tightly aligned strategy, our efforts generated more than **$20 million in pipeline growth** within the first 14 months. Eventually, we concluded the engagement—but the story didn't end there. Several months later, the account team received a call from the company's former chief technology officer (CTO), who had moved to a new organization and requested our support on a new digital transformation initiative. That single reconnection has since resulted in **over $8 million in additional pipeline revenue**—a testament to the lasting impact of a trusted relationship.

In Strategic ABM, it's not just about closing deals—it's about opening doors that stay open long after the campaign ends.

White- Glove Experiences Delivering Results

Starting a conversation with a potential client can feel like navigating unfamiliar territory. When you're aiming to connect with the people who truly matter for your business—those high-value, strategic accounts—simply shouting louder or sending generic messages won't cut it. Think about the difference between a mass e-mail blast and a personal handwritten note; the impact is worlds apart.

This isn't just being polite; it's about providing a very high level of service from the start. White glove means crafting every interaction carefully for a select group of accounts that are particularly valuable. By taking this extra step, businesses can make a strong, lasting impression, show they genuinely understand the challenges these clients face, and importantly, see significant gains on their investment.

When I organized Customer Briefings for the Global IP Network division of NTT Ltd, it wasn't just about selecting the right speakers or curating relevant content—it meant managing every detail, from hotel logistics to meals to entertainment. The goal was to make the experience as memorable as the insights that were shared. It required significant effort, but the results were worth it. Thanks to people like Fernando Costantino and Caroline Staiger, these events evolved into something clients didn't just attend—they looked forward to, often asking, "When's the next one?"

What does this special treatment look like in Strategic ABM? It includes a variety of tailored interactions. Imagine receiving content that speaks directly to your specific situation, or sitting down for a briefing with company leaders who offer insights crafted just for you. I have even gone so far as to create a podcast that was targeted to only one account. We sponsored two of our leading thought leaders in healthcare on a podcast. We worked with the organizer to ensure that the topics discussed were identified pain points of certain ABM identified accounts in the healthcare vertical. We then created targeted advertising to engage those specific accounts with our messaging. I used the content from this 1:Few campaign to customize the messaging to my Strategic ABM accounts. I then had our executive sponsor provide an introduction voice over and cut up the video to showcase specific and identified pain points that we had identified for the account. Finally, I armed the account team with direct links to a hidden, nonindexable website that had additional personalized messaging for the target account. This is how you can go from a personalized piece of collateral to a customized and highly tailored message that speaks to your Strategic ABM account. However, even small things, like a thoughtful gift that shows you've paid attention to their interests, can make a big difference. These actions aren't just nice gestures; insight demonstrates a keen understanding of what keeps your target accounts up at night and can truly resonate with the people making key decisions. For instance, a briefing offering custom insights can directly help clients solve problems they're facing, while a personal gift reminds them you value the connection and understand what they hold as important.

Putting these considerate touches into your strategy for individual accounts can significantly affect how connections grow and drastically effect a customer's journey. When you take the time to figure out what someone likes or what's important to them, you can create moments that feel meaningful and memorable. This kind of effort can lead to clients being more loyal and more likely to speak highly of your company. And yes, this often leads to better business results, like bigger deals and faster sales cycles. It shows that these efforts pay-off in concrete ways.

Again, being able to track effectiveness means setting clear goals from the beginning, identifying what you need to measure, and using the information you gather to improve what you do next time. By doing this, you can justify continuing to invest in these valuable strategies and make them even better over time. To help ensure that we had the right impact for the podcast that we mentioned earlier, we used Urchin Tracking Modules (UTMs) to track traffic to the page, video views and we reviewed new opportunities in our CRM while enquiring of any new interest during regular account team meetings.

Things to Consider as Measurements

If you're looking to put this kind of special attention into action, there are a few things to keep in mind. First, dedicate time to really understand your target account's pain points and what they need. This means doing the research, talking to the people who work with them, and using information you can access to help guide your strategy. Create experiences that are truly unique. Shape how you interact with those target accounts using things like content made just for them, briefings with executives that offer worthwhile thought leadership. Giving gifts that have been carefully chosen. Keep track of your results and the value you're creating. Figure out your goals, track the right things, and use that information to refine your strategy and get better outcomes. Focusing on providing these high-touch experiences as a core part of reaching important accounts allows businesses to build stronger connections, get measurable results, and gain an advantage in the competitive business world today.

Quantifiable Outcomes and ROI from Real Programs

Every marketer should always be asking the same fundamental question: Are my efforts delivering value? In the focused world of ABM, particularly when you concentrate intensely on just a few companies. Showing the return on that focused investment, the ROI, is extremely helpful to understand if the work is effective. While some ABM takes a broader, more automated path, Strategic ABM zeros in with customized, high-touch approaches, especially valuable when you're dealing with large businesses and significant deals.

The payoff from this intense focus shows up directly in the revenue from those target accounts. Seeing revenue increase with your target accounts is the clearest sign that your Strategic ABM efforts are working. When resources are directed toward accounts with the highest potential, the effect can be substantial and easy to track. Think of marketing here less like broadcasting and more like a specialist adviser, working closely with the account team, shaping strategy together, and creating content designed specifically for the key decision-making stakeholders. The value generated by Strategic ABM comes from its accuracy and depth. You are a surgeon, and the precision is what makes this technique effective for driving significant business outcomes.

Another measure of how well things are going in Strategic ABM is how quickly deals move forward or the deal lifecycle. Speeding up the time it takes to close opportunities in these important accounts leads to faster revenue, smoother operations, and making the most of your resources. Speed is extremely important in Strategic ABM. When you engage personally and provide content and thought leadership customized specifically for a small audience, it helps build confidence and trust with those crucial decision makers, helping things progress more swiftly.

Looking beyond the initial sale, the long-term value a customer brings is a vital measurement in Strategic ABM, also known as the CLV (Figure 8.2). A higher CLV signals stronger, more enduring relationships and promises future revenue streams. Businesses absolutely must keep CLV in mind as they plan their 1:1 ABM campaigns. By providing experiences and content made just for them, companies can build lasting ties with significant accounts, driving growth and revenue for years to come. Also, I believe that excluding Strategic ABM accounts from general marketing content is imperative to ensure target audiences are not shown irrelevant content.

Ultimately, the total revenue generated from your efforts is how the investment's return is measured. This provides a clear picture of the program's success. By keeping track of how revenue grows, how fast deals close, and the long-term value of customers, businesses can see the effectiveness of their ABM activities. This information helps them make choices based on facts to evolve their prowess.

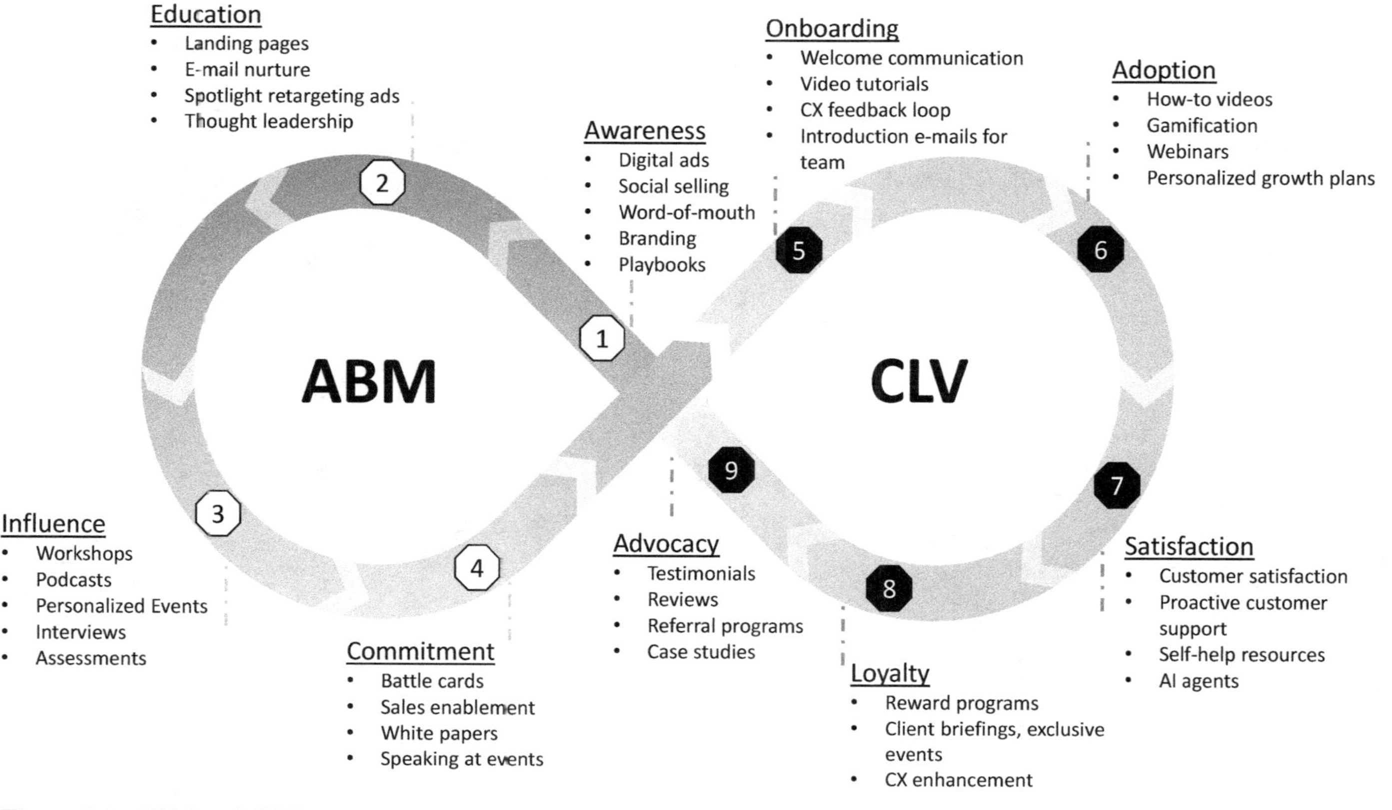

Figure 8.2 ABM and CLV

To measure the return in 1:1 ABM campaigns effectively, some simple practices make a big difference:

- Focus your energy on accounts that offer high potential for revenue. Developing stronger connections and specific content is a top priority.
- Watch revenue growth and the speed of closing deals to see the effectiveness of your ABM campaigns.
- Think about long-term customer value. Building lasting connections with target accounts helps secure future income.
- Use what your data tells you. Let insights guide your 1:1 ABM planning and make program performance more efficient.
- Clearly define additional KPIs, how you will track and weigh the outcomes. Will you create campaigns in your CRM and then drop them into the Primary Campaign Source under opportunities? Will you allow for 100 percent of attribution or only a percentage of the annual contract value (ACV) or total contract value (TCV) revenue? You should consider all of these things as you begin your ABM journey.

By following these straightforward approaches and focusing on the return and the numbers that show performance, you can help to set your Strategic ABM program up for success. With a clear picture of the return and the important numbers, companies can fine-tune their 1:1 ABM campaigns, boosting revenue, closing deals faster, and increasing CLV.

Overcoming the Challenges

Bringing Strategic ABM to life requires more than just initial design; it demands effective execution across several critical dimensions. Attaining support from senior leadership is foundational, providing essential resources and ensuring organizational unity. A solid bedrock of accurate, centralized data proves indispensable, driving personalized experiences and deep insights while safeguarding privacy. Careful planning and judicious resource allocation, often starting with focused trials and prioritizing accounts with the highest potential, enable efficient operation.

Upholding consistent quality in every account interaction maintains trust and perceived value. Finally, dealing with accounts calls for constant vigilance, flexibility, readiness to pivot, and the ability to reassess and adapt strategies as situations shift or progress slows.

Securing and Maintaining Executive Buy-In and Sponsorship

The one thing that every single successful ABM program has, senior leadership in your corner. Call it executive support, top-down backing, upstream buy-in, whatever feels right—this is the critical ingredient for success. Without it, even the most well-designed ABM plans often find themselves adrift, starved of the necessary resources and organizational harmony required to make a real impact. Programs can falter; results fall short of potential. And eventually finding yourself phased out from the company.

Securing this backing requires a clear demonstration of purpose. You need to articulate precisely how Strategic ABM doesn't just sit alongside the business strategy but actively contributes to it. This means showing the path to tangible outcomes: How does it help increase the money coming in, make customers happier, or carve out a larger slice of the market? Connecting 1:1 ABM campaigns directly to these overarching business objectives lays a solid groundwork for earning support from the people at the top.

At the same time, you also need to show other marketing departments that you're not a threat to their way of life. Even though I am a massive fan of ABM, I have never been so naïve as to think that this would take the place of Lead Generation, Go-to-Market (GTM), Events, Branding, or other established departments. ABM works at a different stage of the funnel than these areas of marketing. They do different things. And making them aware that you're not going to replace them is very important to having those departments buy into and support your efforts.

Part of making this case involves painting a picture of what success looks like. To accomplish this, you need to craft specific financial outlooks for targeted accounts, detailing the expected upsides, and illustrating how these focused efforts translate into higher revenue. Providing a clear sense of the potential financial gain gives executives a concrete reason to believe in ABM.

Keeping key leadership engaged requires consistent, open dialogue about the goals and progress of the target account. Regular updates on how things are moving, celebrating wins with specific accounts, and noting key achievements reached keeps them informed. This transparency ensures their continued involvement and support throughout the entire process. You and your team will need to become comfortable communicating with your own senior leadership as well. This can also work to your benefit as many executive sponsors that are engaged with ABM efforts tend to become advocates for your program going forward.

To maintain that vital executive backing, you must show concrete results and make clear how these initiatives add to the bottom line. This involves diligently tracking relevant data points—how engaged are the target accounts, what percentage are moving forward, how is revenue growing as a direct result? Presenting these metrics regularly demonstrates the program's value. Showing the measurable impact of Strategic ABM on the business helps solidify ongoing support from leadership.

Finally, including executives in significant interactions with target accounts as executive sponsors, when appropriate, helps ensure everyone is connected and informed. This can involve inviting them to participate in important client discussions, providing them with updates on how specific high-value accounts are progressing, or seeking their thoughts on strategies for those accounts. Drawing executives into these specific interactions helps ensure their objectives stay aligned with the aims of your ABM program.

Data Management, Accuracy, and Accessibility for Account Insights

Repeatedly, we've discussed how data is key when building successful account-based management programs for all your marketing endeavors, including Programmatic, ABM Lite, Deal Acceleration, and especially in 1:1 ABM instances. Accurate, accessible data isn't just helpful; it's the engine that drives personalization and customization, allowing you to truly see each account for who they are. It provides the understanding needed to craft messages that resonate, sales approaches that land—and ultimately fuel business expansion. Without a solid data foundation, even the most creative marketing and ABM ideas remain just ideas, lacking the insight to make them effective.

For clarity you need to gather all of the previously stated pieces—and those pieces are often scattered. Account data tends to live across multiple platforms: marketing automation systems, sales enablement tools, social channels, and every touchpoint in between. Integrating this information into a single, coherent view isn't just helpful—it's essential. A centralized data source ensures that everyone across sales and marketing is aligned, working from the same set of insights, and delivering a consistent message.

Lack of clarity tends to lead to delays and a total lack of confusion of who is responsible for what when trying to achieve the goals and desired outcomes of the organization. I once dealt with an issue with access issues with a CRM that made it nearly impossible to understand what the account team was collectively working toward. The positive from this experience was that we increased our regular cadence and our ABM and account team became more closely aligned than ever. This was naturally a short-term solution for a problem that would eventually be corrected. This is just another example of how an ABMer needs to be agile and constantly paying attention to the world around them.

Having access to data is only part of the equation. If data isn't maintained, it quickly loses its value. Records become outdated, duplicates creep in, and inaccuracies start to compound. That's why it's critical to implement regular data hygiene practices—validating entries, running audits, and correcting inconsistencies. Auditing your current data forms the foundation for any successful ABM program and ensures you're acting on insights that you can trust.

As you collect and centralize data, another critical aspect comes into sharp focus: privacy. Leading a Strategic ABM campaign means handling confidential account information, and privacy is crucial. Following rules like the GDPR and others is essential not just for legal compliance but for building credibility with your target accounts. This means having clear rules about how data is handled, getting clear permission when needed, and being open about your data practices. "Trust is hard-earned, easily lost, and difficult to reestablish,"[26] said Carol Folt, president of Southern California. Privacy includes handling sensitive account data that has catastrophic ramifications if not safe guarded properly.

[26]Harmeling (2021).

Making sure you're allowed to use the data you've gathered is the next step. Sales and marketing need the right tools and the ability to see and use account information to execute campaigns. Providing this access empowers them to act on insights. Of course, this must be balanced with sensible data rules and security measures to keep everything protected.

What does it look like to take all of this and turn it into a play? It looks like being smart about where your account data lives—creating that single source of truth everyone references. It means regularly validating and auditing that data, so it stays reliable. It means always being mindful of data privacy rules and being transparent. It means giving your teams the tools they need to work with the data. And it means constantly looking at what the data tells you, using those insights to guide your ABM plays to help and improve how your programs perform. By focusing on the quality, accessibility and governance of your data, you will create the necessary conditions for effective 1:1 ABM campaigns that will move the needle.

Resource Allocation, Budgeting, and Bandwidth Management

If you approach ABM as a fundamental shift in how your business generates revenue—especially further down the funnel—you'll start to see meaningful results. But if you treat it like just another marketing tactic in the Marketing Mix, chances are, you'll miss the mark. Think of it like golf, ABM isn't your long game—it's your short game. This isn't about blasting messages down the fairway. It's about precision, patience, and well-placed shots that count.

Succeeding with Strategic ABM requires more than just a new mindset. It demands a deliberate and disciplined approach to how you allocate your always-limited resources.

Resource allocation is the fuel behind a successful program. It's what enables you to identify high-value accounts, craft customized strategies, and ultimately drive measurable impact. Without the right investment—in time, tools, people, and platforms—it's impossible to sustain meaningful engagement with the accounts that matter most.

Now, I know I've mentioned a range of tools and resources throughout this book, and no one expects you to secure them all. My goal has been to paint a picture of what a fully resourced Strategic ABM program should look like. Not as a checklist—but as inspiration. Use it to guide your approach and shape what works best for your team, your goals, and your organizational reality.

Planning Where Resources Go

Thinking carefully about resource allocation from the outset ensures that people, budget, and technology are directed appropriately. This upfront planning helps to sidestep common pitfalls that can derail ABM efforts before they even get started. It means taking a step back and looking at what resources you currently have, figuring out where the gaps are, and understanding what investments will be needed to genuinely support your ABM initiatives. It may also mean looking at what other teams have for funding and how you can partner or work with them to tap into those funds.

A well-structured resource plan allows businesses to begin modestly and increase their efforts over time. You don't need to go all in on day one. Starting with a focused, manageable pilot program provides a practical way to test your assumptions about budget needs and evaluate the workload requirements for your team.

Beginning with a sample size allows you to refine your resource strategy and get a real sense of whether your Strategic ABM approach is viable before rolling it out more broadly. This step helps surface potential issues early, giving you the chance to make the necessary adjustments. It makes for a smoother implementation later. By running a pilot, you gather data to inform decisions about how resources should be allocated moving forward. You may also consider lower hanging fruit accounts with strong relationships and existing executive engagement, if they are already Client Briefing members. This allows you to showcase the art of the possible and make learning from any mistakes easier.

Focusing on What Matters Most

Identifying and prioritizing accounts based on their strategic importance and potential for generating significant business is foundational for ABM. This means directing dedicated resources toward those accounts that truly warrant the attention and customizing your marketing activities to meet their particular needs. When starting out, always consider the 80/20 rule to select accounts for ABM.

Achieving this requires a blend of resources. Using a mix of internal team members and external partners to provide flexibility. Balancing your in-house expertise with specialized outside help offers a path to scalability as your ABM efforts grow.

This combination of internal and external resources will allow you to draw on the strengths of both. Your internal team possesses deep knowledge of your products, services, and company culture. External partners, on the other hand, often bring specialized skills and the ability to quickly scale resources up or down as needed. Combining these assets builds a resilient ABM strategy capable of delivering results.

Making the Most of Your Team's Time

Implementing automation wherever possible is vital for maximizing your team's capacity. It frees up valuable time and resources that can then be dedicated to high-value, personalized interactions and the kind of connection-building that all forms of ABM require. This involves using technology to streamline marketing activities, reduce manual tasks, and improve the efficiency of your ABM initiatives overall. Also, consider the hiring of ABM agencies that can assist you in some of the heavier lifts and automate your initial process to stand up an account.

By automating routine work, your team can focus on developing messages and meaningful connections and listening to the actual needs of sales that help to build target accounts, which will drive revenue growth through properly focused efforts.

Getting resource allocation right involves a considered combination of people, defined processes, and supporting technology. This mix is necessary for managing all ABM programs efficiently and achieving your organization's desired outcomes. It requires continuously monitoring and evaluating how resources are being used and making changes as needed to ensure everything stays aligned with the overall business goals. This considered approach to resource allocation is what drives account momentum and contributes directly to long-term ABM success.

Maintaining Consistency and Quality with High-Touch Interactions

When engaging directly with specific, high-value strategic accounts, the margin for error shrinks considerably. Unlike broadcasting a message to thousands, speaking to a select few demands precision. You will learn to rely heavily on the perception of value and the confidence those target accounts place in your efforts. Any misstep, any hint of inconsistency, can unravel the careful work invested in building that connection. You will become very protective of your accounts and your account teams as you develop your Strategic ABM program.

Maintaining this elevated standard requires vigilance. This is where the idea of strict quality control becomes not just helpful but vital. Think of it as protecting the investment you've made in identifying and pursuing these accounts. A single e-mail with a typo, a phone call that lacks key context, or a social media interaction that feels off-brand can quickly diminish the perceived care you've put in to establish trust, and you will find it more difficult to reestablish. Doing this risks damaging your standing and the reputation of your organization and wasting the time and investment you've already made.

To ensure consistency and quality across all points of contact—whether e-mail, phone, social channels, or in person—many find structure in what we call playbooks. These are detailed guides, outlining the specific steps and considerations for each type of interaction. Having a clear playbook means anyone on the team can execute a touchpoint correctly, maintaining a standardized, high-quality delivery. For example, an e-mail nurture playbook might cover everything from crafting effective subject lines to structuring the message body and planning follow-up actions. These playbooks help to showcase what's best and prevent variations that could confuse or dilute your message. That doesn't mean you will have all the answers in these playbooks, but they can help in bringing on new ABMers who will be responsible for their own accounts.

Beyond establishing these guides, a thorough review process for communications heading out the door is essential. Before an e-mail goes out, before a social post targeting a specific executive is published, it warrants careful scrutiny. This review confirms the messaging aligns with the account's particular situation and needs, and that it accurately reflects your brand's voice. Checking and refining materials ensures each interaction feels genuinely tailored to the account and its decision makers, which naturally increases the likelihood they will engage.

Regular checks on how these activities perform are also key. By auditing engagement data—like e-mail open rates, click-through rates, or how often accounts respond—you gain insight into what's working and what needs adjustment. This allows you to pinpoint areas needing attention and make choices based on what the data shows, refining your strategy for better outcomes.

Also, be aware and constantly test timing and staggering of messaging to make the most out of your resources. You probably won't be able to create forty e-mails a year for one account. But you could create six e-mails that are staggered to go out over three months by breaking up the cycle. And then based on opens you could look to create additional prompts and sample other e-mails that the Lead Generation or other departments are using.

Ensuring high-quality delivery and building account confidence involves putting these practices into action. Develop those specific guides for interactions. Put in place checks and balances before sending anything out. Regularly examine engagement data for consistency and areas to improve. Use data and performance numbers to guide decisions about quality. Continuously refine your approach based on these observations. Organizations that prioritize these aspects often see tangible results; one target account observed a significant increase in executive engagement metrics simply by adopting a more thoughtful, tailored approach to their messaging. It demonstrates the direct payoff of focusing on quality and consistent execution in high-touch ABM.

Adapting to Account Dynamics, Changes, and Setbacks

The only thing that remains constant is change.[27]

Heraclitus, Greek Philosopher

---

[27]Heraclitus (1925).

If you've spent any time growing a business, you know that's not just a quote—it's a daily reality. Business landscapes shift: companies merge, priorities realign, stakeholders come and go, and external forces disrupt even the best-laid plans. In Strategic ABM, success doesn't come from building a rigid plan—it comes from your ability to adapt when the ground shifts beneath you. Sometimes I joke that ABM actually stands for "Always Be Moving."

Staying closely attuned to what's happening inside your target accounts is essential. As internal dynamics evolve and market conditions change, your strategy must also evolve. This means consistently monitoring developments and being ready to pivot so that your efforts remain aligned with the account's current goals and challenges.

Sometimes, your strongest internal advocates leave. When a key contact moves on, it can temporarily unsettle your progress. But it also opens the door to reassess the relationship. What are the account's needs today as opposed to yesterday? How have their goals shifted? Building new relationships is an opportunity to listen, reset, and sometimes uncover new, previously hidden opportunities. In fact, new stakeholders often bring fresh energy and different perspectives that can benefit the account—and your engagement.

You'll encounter setbacks. Campaigns stall. Deals slow down. But setbacks aren't dead ends—they're invitations to reassess. By understanding what caused the slowdown, adjusting your approach, and maintaining open lines of communication, you can often get things moving again. That might mean rearticulating your value proposition, reframing your messaging, or addressing a different pain point entirely.

> "There are no mistakes, only happy accidents."
> —Bob Ross

Adaptability is one of the most powerful tools in a Strategic ABMer's toolkit. Your ability to adapt to shifting account needs, decision makers, and timelines can make the difference between stagnation and renewed momentum. Routinely reviewing and recalibrating your strategy ensures your ABM efforts stay relevant and impactful.

To stay nimble and responsive in the face of change, consider these best practices:

- Track account activity continuously: Stay on top of personnel shifts, business restructuring, and new market pressures.
- Adapt early and often: Don't wait for big disruptions—adjust your approach proactively as smaller signals emerge.
- Communicate clearly and consistently: Keep channels open and responsive so that you can stay aligned with evolving expectations.
- Review and refine regularly: Make ongoing improvements based on current insights, not assumptions.

ABM thrives on connection—and connection requires awareness. By staying agile and responsive, you can turn change into momentum and setbacks into strategic gains.

CHAPTER 9

Measuring Impact and Scaling for the Future

Measuring ROI and Performance Metrics

76 percent of marketers see a higher ROI with ABM than any other marketing strategy.[28]

Bev Burgess

True success in Strategic ABM goes beyond simple metrics. It demands a deliberate approach, one that directly connects your efforts to the organization's most important aims. This requires determining how ABM contributes to financial outcomes, tracking how target accounts interact and assessing their overall health, and measuring the financial return on your investment. Making sense of performance also means communicating results clearly so all stakeholders understand the value you've created.

Defining Success Metrics and KPIs

Measuring success isn't a matter of pulling a standard marketing report template off the shelf. It calls for a customized method built from several angles. This isn't about ticking boxes; it's about critically thinking about the work you do and how it affects the things the business cares about most. Think revenue, market share, or how strong your ties are with key accounts. Every action taken should contribute to the organization's ultimate financial well-being.

The first step involves aligning your measurement points to the overarching business objectives. This means defining the specific signals that

[28]Burgess (2025).

will tell you if your 1:1 ABM campaign efforts work and are hitting the mark. The typical big picture aims for a business often involves boosting income, gaining more ground in the market, and deepening connections with important accounts. When you take the time to correctly connect your ABM goals to connect your outcomes, you ensure your energy goes toward driving results that will affect long-term outcomes.

Understanding exactly where revenue comes from is a critical piece of the puzzle. Get clear on how your efforts influence income, both directly and indirectly. Direct influence comes from revenue generated straight from campaigns—the deals closed because of a specific action. Indirect influence relates to revenue impacted by the work, even if it didn't cause a direct conversion—things like increased awareness or higher levels of engagement. Example, showcasing your leadership team as thought leaders to key accounts via blogs, publishing on industry popular websites.

A well-defined process for attributing revenue will allow you to show the true business impact of your ABM activity. No matter what method you choose to credit different marketing steps along the path to a deal. Make sure that it will provide a picture of how various interactions contribute to closed/won status. In a perfect world, Lead Generation, GTM, Event Management, and ABM would all work together to help develop a unified picture of the customer's journey. Sadly, that is not the case as many marketing departments tend to spend much of their time fighting for credit over influenced versus sourced pipeline and fail to focus on how to effectively accomplish this goal.

Pay close attention to how members of the key buying groups engage is the next step. This involves watching interactions and how content is used to understand how the people you're targeting are interacting with your brand. Consider using observational qualitative market research. Looking at things like how many e-mails are opened and clicked, website visits, activity on social channels, and who is downloading or viewing your content gives you clues. By following these indicators, you get insights into what's effective and what isn't, letting you tweak your approach as needed.

Checking in on the strength of your relationships and the overall health of accounts should happen regularly. This involves getting a feel for how satisfied key clients are and how likely they are to advocate for you, often through direct feedback. Tools that gauge customer satisfaction or willingness to promote, along with specific account health indicators, can be useful. Evaluating how strong these ties are helps identify areas that need attention and allows for decisions based on facts to improve your ABM methods.

Remember, it's critical to put in place a well-rounded collection of measurements. This means including metrics that capture both the numbers and the less tangible aspects of 1:1 ABM performance. Quantitative metrics include things you can count, pipeline size, conversion percentages, deal value, and revenue itself. Qualitative metrics touch on feelings and perceptions: how satisfied clients are, their willingness to recommend you, and overall account well-being. Using a mix gives you a full picture of how your 1:1 ABM campaign is going.

And don't worry if they are not all in place when you begin your ABM journey. Like many things, your understanding will evolve overtime. The absolute worst thing an ABM program can do is not start due to fear. Once you begin to doubt your process, it's difficult to get back on track.

Forecasting ABM Revenue and Growth

You need to remember that a big part of the ABM process is understanding what is important to and getting the attention of your target audience. Are they seeing what you send? Do they care about what you say? To answer these questions, you need a way to gauge interest, a way to measure what engagement looks like for these specific accounts.

Let's set some clear definitions of what counts as engagement. These are the signals accounts give that show they have interest in your brand or product. They show up across different points where you connect with your target audience. For Strategic ABM, these measurements help us see how accounts interact with us.

Starting out, define the key engagement metrics that make sense for your organizations' aims. What signals honestly matter?

- **Time spent on a page**: How long someone stays on a web page or with a piece of content. What are acceptable bounce rates? Can you glean any insights from where users click on the page?

- **Resources downloaded or accessed:** How many times an account opens or downloads a document, like an e-book or report. Many companies choose to put things behind walled content, where you must complete a form before you can access the desired content. Because Strategic ABM is targeting such a niche and identified audience, this tends to drive down numbers and isn't suggested as best practice. However, you can incorporate tools and platforms from vendors such as DemandScience to attempt to capture Exit Intent to capture interest.
- **Meeting engagement:** How many members of your target account regularly join presentations. How engaged are they during quarterly reviews? Are they providing productive feedback? How active are they during client calls?

Having clear definitions of engagement ensures you measure the same thing every time for every account. This gives a consistent picture. This will also allow for you to have better depth of account understanding and expectations as you scale your Strategic ABM practice over time.

Getting a deeper sense of how an account engages means putting a system in place to score engagement signals across channels. This system should give you a single picture of account actions and their intent to purchase. This allows you to follow engagement amounts and to draw direct lines from engagement to purchasing. This deeper understanding proves paramount when streamlining other areas of your marketing divisions.

When building this scoring system, keep these points in mind:

- **Track across multiple platforms:** Look at e-mail, social media, website visits, and more.
- **Score with weight:** Give different scores to various engagement signals based on how much they matter to your business aims.
- **Score by account**: Score engagement at the account level, not just for one person. This gives a view of the whole account's activity.

Watching account engagement amounts and seeing the quality of connections is needed to show if personalized efforts work. It also helps you figure out if content needs changes and if your plan needs adjusting.

When you look at interaction quality, think about talks that truly matter and points of contact that have real influence, not just how many there are.

- **Conversation quality:** Judge how good conversations are with accounts, including how involved they seem and their level of interest. There should always be a human component of ensuring that they are actual decision makers.
- **Influential points:** Find the points of contact that have a big effect on deciding to buy, such as asking for a demonstration or signing up for an on-site workshop.

Getting feedback from accounts will help to fill any gaps in the numbers. Just another example of the importance of the relationship between the ABMer and the account team.

- **Understand need:** Get a clearer idea of why accounts are connecting with your brand. Always start with the "Why." To be able to create impactful content you need to understand your client. Simon Sinek's "Start With Why" philosophy centers on understanding the purpose, cause, or belief that inspires an organization to do what it does. In ABM, this idea becomes a foundation for authentic connection. Rather than focusing solely on what you sell or how you deliver it, starting with the "why" allows you to communicate your deeper purpose and align it with your target account's goals and vision. This not only strengthens trust but also ensures your messaging and ABM 1:1 campaign will speak directly to the heart of what matters most to your audience.
- **Find solutions:** See what issues or interests accounts are trying to solve. Learn about your target account's pain points by doing regular research and discovering opportunities where your organization can create solution-based outcomes.

Finally, check and update your engagement metrics and scoring system regularly. This keeps them right for changing business aims and account needs.

- **Check often:** Set-up times with account teams to look at engagement metrics and the scoring system to make sure they are still helpful and work well. I find that weekly or biweekly meetings are best for this level of engagement. It also allows you to see if there are any changes that need immediate attention.
- **Make regular updates:** Adjust your standardized engagement metrics and scoring systems when needed to show changes in business aims or account needs. Regularly refreshing ads, content, and other items are important. It creates better trust and more honest conversations and understanding between the account and the needs of the account team.

These steps will help you to set-up a way to measure engagement that gives a single view of account activity and interest levels. This lets you make your 1:1 ABM campaign better and get the results that will make a difference.

Measuring Pipeline Influence and Revenue Contribution

There always comes a moment in ABM when you must ask the difficult question: Is this working? And if it is, how? Pinpointing the true impact of your ABM efforts presents a different kind of puzzle compared to traditional marketing. You need to be willing to always be doing postmortems to understand the why. Again, going back to always be willing to take an honest look at the work that you are doing and if it is moving the needle.

That work often shows its value long before a contract is signed. We often fixate on the final number, which is certainly vital, but it doesn't tell the whole story of how ABM helped to get us there. ABM isn't just there at the finish line; it's involved much earlier, helping shape interest and accelerate the path forward. And it should be there much longer afterward in the relationships that have developed across the account team and the key decision makers. Thinking about ABM's influence means looking at how it helps create and move potential deals through the early stages of the sales cycle. This way, we get a clearer picture of its overall contribution. In many cases we used a combination of types of ABM for our most successful accounts. We initially engaged the account through the Deal Acceleration process and then transitioned over to a Strategic or 1:Few ABM model.

Tracing ABM's contribution requires acknowledging every point of interaction. A single deal doesn't usually happen because of one e-mail or one meeting. It's the cumulative effect of multiple engagements across time. Effective measurement means seeing the whole picture—understanding how different ABM activities connect with buyers throughout their decision-making process and recognizing that many small influences add up to a big outcome. To really see this multipoint influence clearly, you need tools that can track contributions from various activities. This is where models designed to look at multiple points of contact come into play. These models help assign value to the different interactions that happen along the way, including all those specific ABM touches. These tools need to be able to be adopted so that it can develop with your ABM process.

Then you need to consider internal comparisons. What happens with accounts where you did apply a dedicated ABM focus? By looking at groups that received the ABM treatment alongside groups that served as a baseline, you can start to isolate the specific lift or difference that ABM made. Is it all just a placebo effect? Do the account teams focus more and work harder because they are being given personalized marketing support? Doing comparisons help quantify the incremental gain from your targeted efforts.

So, how do you put this into practice? A few guiding ideas come to mind:

- Focus on tracking how your ABM activities influence accounts at various stages, rather than only looking at direct revenue figures.
- Give credit to ABM for its role in generating and speeding up opportunities early on. Make sure you're attributing the impact of all your ABM actions across every relevant point of contact.
- Look for tools that can track all touch points that account for end-to-end influences on deals.
- Always compare the results of your ABM-targeted accounts against a control group to understand the real difference it makes. This will make sure that you are staying honest with yourself and help to hold you accountable.

Calculating ROI for Strategic Accounts and ABM Programs

Anyone who's ever tried to figure out if a marketing campaign made money knows it can feel like chasing shadows. We throw a budget at initiatives, see some activity—clicks, opens, maybe a lead—but when someone asks the simple question, "Was it worth it?" The answer often gets complicated. This is particularly true in the new world of ABM where the stakes are high, and the targets are few and precious.

To get a real answer, one that everyone from the marketing intern to the CEO can agree on, we need a bedrock principle: a single, crystal-clear understanding of what ROI means for our ABM efforts. Without this unified view, teams work with different assumptions, numbers don't line up, and assessing true impact becomes nearly impossible. It's like trying to build something together when half the crew thinks "measure twice" means check the length, and the other half thinks it means look at the color. A common clear definition is an essential starting point.

Measuring net profit margin (NPM) is one of the most direct ways to assess the financial efficiency of your Strategic ABM program. To calculate it, start with the total revenue generated from your targeted strategic accounts. Subtract the total cost of running your ABM program—including technology, media, content, and personnel—and then divide that figure by your total program spend and multiply your result by one hundred to get the percentage.

The result will reveal how much profit your ABM investment is truly delivering after all expenses are accounted (Figure 9.1).

Applying this consistently, account by account or campaign by campaign, gives you a base concept of how to gauge performance.

Getting to that number means accounting for everything that went into the program. It's more than just ad spend. You must factor in the cost of the people involved—the salaries and benefits for the sales folks, marketers, and customer success teams dedicating time to these accounts. Then there's additional costs like the martech stack: The ABM platform itself, marketing automation tools, and your CRM system aren't free.

$$\text{Net Profit Margin (\%)} = \frac{\text{Net Income}}{\textbf{Total Revenue}} \times 100$$

***Figure 9.1** Formula for net profit margin*

Don't forget the effort and cost of creating personalized and customized content. And, most importantly, any direct marketing spending like targeted ads, e-mail campaigns, or sponsoring an event that your target accounts would attend.

Pinpointing the revenue side requires diligence. You need to track the money coming in from your strategic accounts. The aim is to tie revenue gains directly back to the ABM work whenever possible. This means keeping a close eye on relevant metrics. Looking at e-mail open rates (which can exceed 44 percent in a focused ABM campaign), click-through rates (1:1 ABM campaigns should be shooting for over 50 percent), and ultimately conversion rates help build the case for ABM's influence on the bottom line.

The true value of ABM extends beyond the tangible ROI. Strategic ABM builds something durable. When evaluating the impact, it's necessary to think about the long haul. What's the potential customer value over their entire engagement with your organization? How has the program helped expand business within existing strategic accounts? Recognizing this longer-term impact is vital; Strategic ABM is not really designed for quick wins but for sustained growth, increased understanding of your portfolio and strengthening key client relationships to hopefully develop partnerships. If you are looking for quick wins, then maybe Deal Acceleration is what you should consider.

Sticking to that standard calculation and being diligent about identifying all associated spending, businesses gain the insight needed to make smart decisions about where to invest next and how to refine their marketing approach. This unified view helps ensure everyone understands the financial impact, leading to better ABM planning and improved results.

Reporting and Communicating Results to Stakeholders

Getting people behind a marketing approach can feel like trying to convince a group of skeptics to climb a mountain together. Everyone nods, agrees with the goal at the summit, but getting them to pack their gear, follow the map, and stay the course? That often comes down to how well you communicate the plan and the progress. With ABM, where you're focusing intensely on specific, high-value targets, keeping everyone on the same page isn't just helpful; it's the bedrock of getting the program off the ground and working.

Think about it—your sales teams, leadership, even product development needs to understand what you're doing and why it matters to them. When you communicate consistently, you're not just sharing data; you're building trust and making sure everyone feels like they're part of the effort. This shared understanding keeps people invested and pulling in the same direction toward the program's goals.

Part of building that consistent flow is setting up a regular rhythm for updates. You need a reporting cadence. Maybe that's touching base every week, every two weeks, or once a month. What matters is that it's scheduled and predictable. This structure gives everyone a chance to see what's happening, offer their perspective, and allows you to spot if something needs adjusting before you get too far down the wrong path.

Now, not everyone cares about the same details. The report you share with the executive team probably shouldn't be the same one you give to the marketing team. Leadership might want to see the big picture—how is this affecting the overall business? What's happening with revenue and potential deals? The marketing folks, though, might need the specifics—which campaigns are driving engagement, what content is working? Giving each group the information they need makes the updates relevant and actionable for them.

Sometimes, numbers look like a tangled mess. This is where showing, not just telling, makes a difference. Charts, simple graphs, pictures that tell the story of the data—these things cut through complexity. They make it easier for anyone looking at the report to quickly see successes and understand where things could improve. Visuals help people grasp what's going on without getting lost in spreadsheets. And visual images can be repurposed to both upstream and downstream audiences.

Ultimately, what really resonates with stakeholders, especially those holding the purse strings, isn't how many e-mails were opened or ads were clicked. They want to know how your ABM work is impacting the business's bottom line. Connect your activities to things like potential revenue, actual deals closed, and the value of a customer over time. Frame the marketing efforts in terms of business impact, not just marketing metrics. This is how you demonstrate the real value being created.

To make sure you're keeping everyone informed and engaged with your strategic ABM efforts, here are a few simple principles: Be open and share updates regularly, whether the news is good or bad. Speak plainly; avoid jargon that only marketers understand. I personally always ask for clarification whenever anyone uses a three-letter acronym (TLA). Always tie your actions back to business outcomes—revenue, pipeline, and customer value. Use charts and graphs to simplify complex information. And remember to adjust the level of detail and focus on your reports based on your audience. Sticking to a regular reporting schedule and following these ideas helps ensure everyone is aware and are accountable. This regular sharing of information shows the value the program is bringing, helping gain that crucial support. This can also help in providing ideas and insights to other areas of marketing of how other marketers can adopt your 1:1 ABM experiences to their own areas.

The Future of Strategic ABM and Agentic AI

The way businesses connect with important accounts is constantly changing. To keep up, Strategic ABM must be ready to adapt engagement strategies quickly. This involves building stronger ties through deeper understanding, using intelligent tools to gain insights and work smarter, and being able to show clear impact to ensure continued account growth.

As your strategic ABM approach matures, your impact depends on understanding and adopting new methods to improve account engagement and deliver value. The focus shifts to demonstrating tangible results, ensuring long-term partnerships are solidified through measurable outcomes. With the integration of advanced technologies, businesses can now uncover hidden patterns in account behavior, anticipate client needs proactively, and provide preemptive solutions that strengthen relationships and foster loyalty.

By leveraging intelligent automation and data-driven insights, you can refine targeting and messaging, improve efficiency, and relevance across multiple platforms. This enables you to forecast future client needs, allowing for proactive engagement and solution provision that not only meets but exceeds client expectations.

Emerging Trends in Strategic Account Engagement

Earlier, we stated how it feels like the ground beneath our feet is constantly moving in the world of Strategic ABM. It feels like just as you master one way of connecting with target audiences, everything shifts. This constant movement affects how we engage target accounts and how quickly we adapt to change. What was cutting-edge Strategic ABM yesterday might be standard practice today, or even outdated tomorrow.

As this focused approach to marketing grows, we see a clear push toward using new ideas and tools to truly connect with accounts and build significant value. Think customized versus personalized outreach, how competitors are bringing AI into the mix, and, crucially, cementing the value of what we do with accounts and key decision-making stakeholders.

Customized Versus Personalized Outreach: Making Connections Deeper

Using what we know from data about our accounts, we can create messages and interactions that feel made just for our target audiences. This doesn't just get their attention; it helps build stronger, more meaningful relationships. Recent studies show that when marketers use data analytics and account knowledge to understand what individual target accounts need and like, it allows for customized conversations, even at scale. And we are seeing companies use this to promote and showcase new thought leaders to target audiences. Reinforcing that they have the right solution right now.

Bringing in AI: Smarter Work, Better Insight

Putting AI into ABM changes how companies work with their accounts. Tools powered by AI can look through huge amounts of information, using Large Language Models (LLM) for each account on a large scale. These tools or models help Strategic ABMers, and marketers provide real, measurable value and create more content to their most important accounts.

Agentic AI Agents can be developed to help from the account selection process to assisting in execution of repetitive tasks, letting marketers spend their time on creative thinking and strategic planning. Many organizations have already been adopting Gen AI over the past two years. One common tool is Writer, the Gen AI full-stack platform that can teach or load your brand guidelines and can help to review and create new and compelling content for audiences. This type of early adoption will allow marketers to get out ahead of competitors in this new world of more personalized content creation.

Proving Value: How to Keep Growing

As Strategic ABM becomes more sophisticated, showing how large of an impact your work is creating is getting more attention. For continued growth, companies need to focus on building long-term relationships by showing solid outcomes. This means looking beyond typical marketing numbers to measure how ABM efforts directly affect revenue and how much a customer is worth over time. When marketers do this, they can show why investing in ABM makes sense and ensure leadership continues to support it. I recently heard of an AI risk detection company that tracked the number of engagements of a recent new client win where there were over 45 interactions and only 4 were with Sales. That shows you that as we move toward what tomorrow looks like, that Marketing, specifically ABM, will begin to see itself with a seat at the decision-making table.

The road ahead for Strategic ABM looks like it will involve even more emphasis on using these developing trends to drive account engagement and create value. We'll see continued progress in making personalization more precise, integrating advanced AI capabilities, and keeping a sharp focus on showing real financial results. As leaders get younger, finding new ways to capture their attention and showcase solutions becomes more elusive, not to mention the difficulties of building long lasting and trusted relationships. It will be your job to explain to internal stakeholders that ABM success goes beyond just marketing numbers, focusing on account progress and making sure that leadership recognizes marketers for cultivating the kinds of relationships that lead to growth.

Leveraging AI and Advanced Analytics for Deeper Insights

What does bringing together Gen and Agentic AI and advanced data analysis look like in tomorrow's world? Honestly, I have no clue. I can tell you that it's fundamentally altering the art of the possible. It opens doors to understanding accounts and personalizing messages in ways we could only dreamed of before. By putting these smart tools to work, marketers gain access to data-driven insights that sharpen their focus and refine their message delivery. It allows businesses to move past general campaigns and toward approaches that feel truly tailored and anticipatory. This new way of thinking makes it so all marketers can see and affect business opportunities from end-to-end in a way they couldn't have previously.

Uncovering Hidden Patterns with AI

AI-powered tools have a remarkable ability to sift through vast quantities of information and pick out signals, patterns, and trends that a person simply wouldn't see, no matter how much time they spent digging. This capability gives all marketers a much deeper insight into the companies they wish to target. It allows them to develop plans that are not just based on company size or industry but on actual behavior and digital footprints of stakeholders. Imagine being able to identify the specific people within an account who hold influence, understand their areas of interest, and even pinpoint the exact challenges they are facing. And then taking that further to find other leadership in other companies who have similarities to those stakeholders. AI makes it possible to build highly customized content and messages directly addressing those audiences and then replicating the process to be able to lift and shift the content to other marketing efforts.

Predictive Analytics for Proactive Engagement

Consider the power of knowing what a target account needs before they do. That's the promise of predictive analytics. By looking at past interactions, buying history, and how homogenous accounts have already crafted solutions, these tools can forecast potential opportunities or challenges down the line. This means that you can get ahead of the curve, offering solutions preemptively. Being proactive in this way not only strengthens relationships but significantly improves the chances of successful deals, buyer timelines and will lead to revenue growth. This will allow your account team to establish themselves apart from other suppliers as providing unique insight.

AI-Driven Content Personalization

One person can create customized content for four or five accounts in a manageable way, as in through ABM 1:1 campaigns stated by Bev Burgess. Doing it effectively for dozens, hundreds, or even thousands across different platforms is a different story. This is where AI automation steps-in. It automates the process of tailoring content, from e-mails and social updates to website experiences, based on account data and individual actions. This drastically improves both the speed and the relevance of communications, making sure every interaction feels designed specifically for that account. The goal is ensuring that each touchpoint is meaningful and increases the likelihood of conversion and revenue generation.

In several years from now we could see the smarter B2B organizations shifting market budgets around and moving away from Lead Gen and over to 1:Few and Strategic ABM practices for two to three years at a time. And then shifting back over to top-of-funnel marketing tactics after they've increased their relationships with existing accounts and created an extensive amount of content that can be shifted upstream to the top of the marketing funnel.

Forecasting Future Client Needs

Advanced analytics takes the ability to look ahead even further. By analyzing historical data alongside market trends and account behavior, companies can forecast future needs with greater accuracy. This provides a clear view of potential opportunities and challenges, allowing marketing teams to build strategies that address client requirements before they even become pressing issues. This proactive approach helps solidify client connections and build lasting loyalty.

Laying the Groundwork for Sustained Growth

Bringing AI and advanced analytics into ABM isn't just about improving current efforts; it's about building a solid foundation for long-term success and the ability to scale your efforts. Using tools and platforms enables businesses to adopt a more anticipatory and tailored method for connecting with accounts, which directly contributes to revenue growth and improves client satisfaction. As the methods for reaching customers continue to change, integrating AI and analytics will become increasingly essential for companies aiming to maintain a competitive edge.

Balancing Scale with High-Touch Principles

Anyone who has successfully built something worthwhile understands that growth introduces new challenges. What worked brilliantly when you were small, nimble, and focused on just a handful of target accounts suddenly feels strained as your world expands. Can you continue to keep that intensely personal, one-on-one connection you had? Keeping that feeling alive while also handling more accounts, more conversations, and more complexity becomes the central puzzle. This isn't just about doing more of the same; it's about maintaining that high level of individual attention as things grow. If you're in the trenches and doing this correctly then you'll be excited for every new account, defend every existing account and silently mourn every account you offboard.

Sustaining success in ABM when you're targeting specific individuals within specific companies requires a very careful balance. You need to expand your efforts without sacrificing the tailored interactions that made them effective in the first place. The pitfall of slipping into generic communications, defeats the entire purpose of a Strategic ABM approach.

To grow intelligently, you can't just water down your methods. You need to adapt your personal touch. Think about developing repeatable steps and clear processes that let your teams handle growth with intention. Using smart ways to reuse content, adapting it slightly for each target, and ensuring everyone on the team is on the same page. This helps keep things relevant and sharp, even as you scale up.

Smart technology is key here. Automation isn't about replacing people; it's about giving them superpowers. By automating routine tasks and using what data tells you, your teams can spend their time on the interactions that truly matter—those high-value moments that build trust and connections. It's about finding the sweet spot where efficiency meets genuine human understanding. Technology supports people, allowing for both speed and sensitivity.

Speaking of data, understanding what's working and what isn't is the bedrock for making smart choices, both in ABM and life. You need to constantly look at how your strategies are performing. Analyzing the information and performing regular testing helps you tweak and improve your approach, so you build value over the long-term. This means prioritizing thoughtful development rather than just chasing quick wins. Again, if the focus is quick wins, then Deal Acceleration is what you want to utilize. And realize that there is no wrong way to begin your ABM journey, as we discussed in Chapter III: Understanding the Core of 1:1 ABM. And Deal Acceleration accounts can transform into Strategic ABM accounts once you have the necessary quick wins or initial deal. However, with Strategic ABM, the focus remains on building strong connections and understanding the nuance needs of each target account.

Giving your teams what they need to keep those high-touch interactions going is critical. Provide them with the necessary training, tools, and support. When people feel capable and supported, they can focus on cultivating those vital connections with target accounts and the individuals within them. Focusing on building those strong bonds and understanding accounts is what drives both deeper connections and lasting expansion, turning you from a vendor to a trusted adviser.

What does this look like in practice?

- Regularly examine your approach, adjusting to ensure lasting value and account expansion.
- Equip your teams to deliver highly personal experiences, keeping the focus on cultivating strong bonds and understanding account subtleties.
- Apply smart technology to allow for personalized outreach at scale, supporting human insight and activity.
- Put planned development ahead of seeking rapid results, prioritizing long-term value and account growth.

By keeping these ideas in mind, focusing on that balance between expansion and keeping things personal, organizations can continue to succeed with their specific account efforts, creating stronger connections and achieving lasting growth.

Integrating 1:1 ABM with Other Marketing and Sales Strategies

Starting to build a Strategic ABM program often feels like standing at the base of a mountain. You know the peak is the ultimate goal—significant business growth—but the path isn't a single, straight forward line. It involves navigating various terrains, each requiring specific tools and approaches. When it comes to creating customized strategies like 1:1 ABM, viewing it as a solo climb misses the point entirely. The real power of Strategic ABM unfolds when it's woven into the broader fabric of your overall marketing and sales efforts. Thinking of 1:1 ABM in isolation is like trying to paddle a boat by yourself; you need to find people who can work together to row in the same direction to help reach your destination.

Consider how Strategic ABM initiatives interact with your wider marketing campaigns. There's a fundamental need to connect these pieces. When the intensely focused outreach of a 1:1 ABM campaign isn't coordinated with your larger marketing activities you risk sending mixed messages. Picture, if you will, a target account seeing a highly customized message from your ABM team one day and then a generic advertisement the next. You need to pull your messaging in tight. Aligning messaging and content ensures the experience is consistent and what you are conveying is unified. It's about creating a single, coherent voice that speaks directly to target account's needs, whether through a broad campaign or a specific ABM play. That is why it is important to exclude Strategic ABM accounts from broader marketing efforts.

Just as crucial is the connection between 1:1 ABM strategy and your sales approach. For account engagement to be truly unified and effective, marketing and sales must operate in concert. This isn't just about being friendly; it's about sharing goals, using the same insights about target accounts, and coordinating actions. When marketing delivers tailored messages via ABM, sales need to be ready to follow-up with equally relevant conversations. This combined effort allows for more efficient and targeted engagement, which directly impacts conversion rates and contributes to revenue generation. Without this link, marketing's careful groundwork can be wasted by a misaligned sales interaction.

A significant benefit of executing 1:1 ABM campaigns are the depth of understanding it provides about your most valuable accounts. These initiatives generate specific data on how target accounts behave, what content they engage with, and where their priorities lie. This information isn't just useful for the ABM team; it offers valuable insights that can refine other marketing strategies. By analyzing engagement patterns and preferences identified through 1:1 ABM, marketers can make data-driven adjustments to broader campaigns, improving overall marketing performance. It's a feedback loop where insights from the specific inform and optimize the general.

Making all this work requires constant communication and collaboration. The success of 1:1 ABM initiatives depend heavily on the marketing team working closely not only with sales but also with other relevant departments. This coordination ensures everyone is on the same page, pursuing shared objectives, and reducing the likelihood of departments operating in silos. Regular exchanges of information and feedback between teams help identify what's working, what isn't, and where adjustments are needed to optimize the overall strategy for engaging target accounts and driving business outcomes.

The process of integrating ABM builds a foundation that allows you to scale effectively in the future. It's about ensuring that this powerful, focused strategy doesn't just deliver short-term wins but contributes to the long-term health and expansion of your business.

CHAPTER 10

What Does It All Mean?

Tying It All Together

Think of building something great. It's not just about laying the foundation; it's about constantly checking, tweaking, and improving as you go. If you stop paying attention, the structure weakens, the elements shift, and soon, what you built no longer has a solid foundation. ABM works much the same way. For ABM to truly deliver lasting value, the team involved needs to operate with a mindset focused squarely on perpetual learning and refinement.

A successful ABM environment doesn't happen by accident. It begins with nurturing a spirit of curiosity and a willingness to try things out. Encouraging team members to experiment and develop new ways to create meaningful experiences and touchpoints. Let them test different approaches, explore new software or platforms, and kick around novel concepts. Imagine an ABM team wondering about the best way to connect via e-mail. They might launch a few variations of a nurture campaign, each with a slightly different message or call to action. By watching what happens—who opens, who forwards, who clicks—they uncover valuable information about what connects with their target audience and what falls flat. Then they are able to create a behavior-based automation workflow that will be able to be lifted and shifted to larger audiences.

Trying things isn't enough; you need to know if they're working. Regularly reviewing your ABM program performance is vital for spotting potential adjustments. Dig into the numbers, engagement rates, conversion metrics, and pipeline growth. Talk to the account team and others involved, get their perspective and don't be afraid to ask for help. Combining what the data says with what people on the ground observe gives a much clearer picture of how well things are performing, allowing for decisions grounded in fact to guide improvements.

As you learn, capturing those discoveries is essential. Documenting lessons learned and effective methods builds a shared pool of understanding that can guide future ABM initiatives. By recording and distributing this knowledge, the team avoids repeating past errors and builds upon prior wins. This means having regular team meetups with your Strategic ABM team. Discuss topics and techniques with each other and bring other expertise into the conversation to discuss how to better assist your accounts and find opportunities to showcase the team's wins.

Staying current on what's happening in the world of ABM—the latest approaches, the newest tools—is also crucial for sharpening effectiveness and staying ahead. This involves looking into different ways of doing things, exploring new platforms, and testing new methods. Perhaps it's using advanced techniques to customize content or using organizational charts to better grasp target accounts. Staying informed and adapting to changing market conditions keeps the team nimble and effective.

Because accounts and markets are always changing, adapting to those shifting sands and dynamics is necessary for long-term ABM success. The team must recognize this constant change and be ready to respond and adjust. By staying attuned to account needs and market shifts, the ABM team can modify strategies and tactics to remain relevant and impactful.

Ultimately, using the information gathered to guide strategy and drive ongoing refinement is what ensures an ABM program stays flexible and successful. Use data and feedback to find areas where you can improve, test new ideas, and fine-tune existing strategies. Through constant learning and refinement, the ABM team achieves long-term success and delivers significant outcomes.

One Last Thing: Let's be "Clear"

I see the ball in the hoop before it leaves my hand

Anonymous

Throughout this book, I've returned to one word again and again: *clear*. And that's no accident. Because at its core, Strategic ABM is about clarity—of purpose, of vision, of execution.

You need a **clear mindset** that cuts through the noise and complexity. You need **clear goals** that keep you and your team aligned, even when the terrain gets rough. You need **clear expectations** that allow you to collaborate with others and show up with purpose. And most of all, you need **clarity of belief**—in your strategy, your value, and the people you bring along on the journey.

ABM isn't for the faint of heart. It asks you to step into complexity, lead without a map, and show resilience when things don't go according to plan. When I first began my ABM journey, I was told that Strategic ABM was like being the CMO for each of your target accounts. Those mentors were spot on. You become the voice of insight, the architect of experience, the driver of growth.

And to do that well, you must see the outcome *before* it happens. You need to visualize success, even when you're navigating uncertainty. That clarity doesn't mean everything goes perfectly—far from it. But it gives you the confidence to adjust, to regroup, and to keep pushing forward when it matters most.

So, here's my closing thought to you, the reader, the practitioner, the future ABMer:

> *Be clear in your goals. Be clear in your intention. And most importantly, be clear in how much you believe in yourself—and the team around you. Because in ABM, just like in life, clarity is the difference between wandering and winning.*

See the ball in the hoop. Then take your shot.

Bibliography

Adamson, B. 2022. "Traditional B2B Sales and Marketing Are Becoming Obsolete." *Harvard Business Review*, February 1. https://hbr.org/2022/02/traditional-b2b-sales-and-marketing-are-bec oming-obsolete.

Adweek Staff. 2018. "How Do You Advertise to an Ad Agency? Put Up a Billboard Right Across the Street. " Accessed February 13, 2025. https://www.adweek.com/creativity/how-do-you-advertise-ad-agency-put-billboard-right-across-street-159734/.

Bleustein-Blanchet, M. 2015. "Change by Marcel Bleustein-Blanchet." Publicis Brazil. Posted December 15, 2015. YouTube. https://www.youtube.com/watch?v=vNt4Yo9Quv4.

Burgess, B. 2017. *A Practitioner's Guide to Account-Based Marketing*. Kogan Page.

Burgess, B. 2022. *Account-Based Growth: Unlocking Sustainable Value Through Extraordinary Customer Focus*. Kogan Page.

Burgess, B., ed. 2025. *Account-Based Marketing: The Definitive Handbook for B2B Marketers*. Kogan Page.

Conklin, N. 2024. "ABM Won, But It's Not Done Changing The Game." *Forrester*, May 30. Accessed January 23, 2025. https://www.forrester.com/blogs/abm-won-but-its-not-done-changing-the-game/.

Dixon, B. A. 2011. *The Challenger Sale: Taking Control of the Customer Conversation*. Portfolio/Penguin.

Fowler, J. (2017). "You Can Make Your Sales Data a Lot Better with a Little Discipline." *Harvard Business Review*, June 13. Accessed November 17, 2021. https://hbr.org/2017/06/you-can-make-your-sales-data-a-lot-better-with-a-little-discipline.

Goins, J. 2015. *The Art of Work: A Proven Path to Discovering What You Were Meant to Do*. Thomas Nelson.

Harmeling, S. 2021. "Trust Is Hard-Earned, Easily Lost, Difficult to Reestablish—And Key To Absolutely Everything." *Forbes*, November 12. Accessed January 18, 2025. https://www.forbes.com/sites/susanharmeling/2021/11/12/trust-is-hard-earned-easily-lost difficult to reestablish and-key-to-absolutely-everything/.

Heraclitus. 1925. *Diogenes Laërtius: Lives of Eminent Philosophers*. Translated by R. Hicks. Harvard University Press.

IndustryARC. 2024. "ABM Market Set to Reach $3.9 Billion by 2030, Fueled by Rising Adoption of Hyper-Personalized Marketing Strategies." November 20. Accessed September 17, 2025. https://www.industryarc.com/Research/account-based-marketing-(ABM)-Market-800562.

Lindenau, K. 2024. "The Cost of Misalignment: Why Sales & Marketing Need to Get on the Same Page." *Demand Gen Report*, November 27. Accessed May 13, 2025. https://www.demandgenreport.com/industry-news/the-cost-of-misalignment-why-sales-marketing-need-to-get-on-the-same-page/48628/.

Magill, P., and C. Moorman. 2022. "Do Your Marketing Metrics Show You the Full Picture?" *Harvard Business Review*, April 4. https://hbr.org/2022/04/do-your-marketing-metrics-show-you-the-full-picture.

Malhotra, N. K. 2019. *Marketing Research: An Applied Orientation.* 7th ed. Pearson Education.

Mela, C. F. 2021. "Don't Buy the Wrong Marketing Tech." *Harvard Business Review*, July–August. https://hbr.org/2021/07/dont-buy-the-wrong-marketing-tech.

Millman, D. 1980. *Way of the Peaceful Warrior: A Book That Changes Lives.* H. J. Kramer/New World Library.

Mulkeen, D. 2024, December 9. "Let's Talk ABM: 7 Ways to Nurture Your Most Important Customers." *Insights—Strategic ABM*, December 9. Accessed December 10, 2024. https://insights.strategicabm.com/lets-talk-abm-7-ways-to-nurture-customer-abm.

Olennikova, Y. 2023. "What Is 1:1, 1:Few, and 1:Many ABM (With Real-Life Examples)." *N.Rich*, January 20. Accessed November 15, 2024. https://nrich.io/blog/one-to-one-few-many-abm-real-life-examples.

O'Neill, S. 2023. "Sales and Marketing Alignment: Stats and Trends for 2023." *LXA, Learning Experience Alliance*, June 5. Accessed February 3, 2024. https://www.lxahub.com/stories/sales-and-marketing-alignment-stats-and-trends-2023.

Peppers, D. M. 1999. "Is Your Company Ready for One-to-One Marketing?" *Harvard Business Review*, January–February. https://hbr.org/1999/01/is-your-company-ready-for-one-to-one-marketing.

Philip Kotler, N. R. 2006. "Ending the War Between Sales and Marketing." *Harvard Business Review* 84 (7/8): 68–78. https://hbr.org/2006/07/ending-the-war-between-sales-and-marketing.

Roberts, K. 2024. *Lovemarks: The Future Beyond Brands.* PowerHouse Books.

Rogers, D. P. 1993. *The One to One Future: Building Relationships One Customer at a Time.* Currency/Doubleday.

Ross, B. n.d. "The Joy of Painting." quoted as "There are no mistakes, only happy accidents." https://www.businessinsider.com/bob-ross-quotes-to-brighten-your-day-2020-4#we-dont-make-mistakes-just-happy-little-accidents-11.

Shakespeare, W. E. 1992. *Hamlet.* Simon & Schuster.

Sinek, S. 2009. *Start with Why: How Great Leaders Inspire Everyone to Take Action.* Portfolio/Penguin.

Singh, M. 2025. "Economic Trends and Their Impact on B2B Demand Generation in 2025." *Vereigen Media,* October 13. Accessed October, 2025. https://vereigenmedia.com/economic-trends-driving-b2b-demand-generation-2025/#:~:text=Shifting%20Buyer%20Behavior%20in%20a,can%20do%20successful%20demand%20generation.

Tantry, S. 2016. "Making Personalized Marketing Work." *Harvard Business Review,* February 29. https://hbr.org/2016/02/making-personalized-marketing-work.

Taylor, D. A. 1987. "Communication in Interpersonal Relationships: Social Penetration Processes." In *Interpersonal Processes: New Directions in Communication Research,* edited by M. E. Roloff and G. R. Miller. SAGE Publications.

Ziglar, Z. 1977. *See You at the Top.* Pelican Publishing Company.

Zimmer, G. 2021. *I Guarantee It: The Untold Story Behind the Founder of Men's Wearhouse.* Beyond Words (distributed by Simon & Schuster).

About the Author

Sloan Newman is a global marketing practitioner with more than 20 years of experience leading strategic marketing and advertising programs for complex enterprise organizations. He holds dual master's degrees in International Marketing Communications and International Marketing Strategy and has worked across agency and in-house roles in the United States and Europe, including at Microsoft and MSL London.

Sloan's experience spans markets such as the United Kingdom, France, Germany, Brazil, and the Netherlands, supporting accounts generating millions in annual pipeline. He is currently part of an award-winning team that helped develop a strategic ABM framework for a top-three global Internet and IP services company headquartered in Japan.

In addition to his professional work, Sloan conducted qualitative marketing research at the Foster School of Business, completed Agentic AI training through Salesforce's Trailforce, and has lectured at the University of Washington, Western Washington University, and London Metropolitan University. He also served as the youngest president of the Puget Sound American Marketing Association.

He wrote this book to help marketers act as the "CMO of their ABM accounts"—owning strategy, relationships, and long-term growth beyond campaigns and metrics.

Index

Account-Based Marketing (ABM), 26, 147
  accessibility for account insights, 162–164
  account dynamics, 168–170
  accuracy, 162–164
  adapting as change happens, 154
  automation, 166
  bandwidth management, 164–165
  budgeting, 164–165
  buy-in and sponsorship, 161–162
  changes, adapting, 168–170
  consistency and quality, 167–168
  and customer lifetime value, 158–159
  data management, 162–164
  different industry and account scenarios, 152–153
  focusing on what matters most, 165–166
  forecasting revenue and growth, 173–181
  getting support from the top, 154
  getting to know them, 153
  integrating with other marketing and sales strategies, 188–189
  1:1 campaign approach, 148–152, 160
  overcoming challenges, 160–168
  pipeline influence and revenue contribution, 176–177
  quantifiable outcomes, 157–160
  resource allocation, 164–165
  rhetorical triangle, 150–151
  ROI from real programs, 157–160
  setbacks, 168–170
  shared ideas, different worlds, 153
  strategic, 156–158, 160–165, 167, 169, 171
  success is more than just numbers, 154–155
Account dynamics, 168–170
Account expectations, 42–52
Account insights, accessibility for, 162–164
Account intelligence, 45–46
Account research agents, 27
Account teams, 82–86
Accuracy, 162–164
Adamson, Brent, 64
Adaptability, 169
Advocacy, 48
Agentic AI, 26–29, 85, 115, 181–187
Agile, 154
Analytics platforms, 144
Annual contract value (ACV), 160
Artificial intelligence (AI)
  agents, 182–183
  driven content personalization, 185
  forecasting future client needs, 185
  hidden patterns with, 184
  laying groundwork for sustained growth, 185–186
  leveraging, 183–184
  predictive analytics for proactive engagement, 184
Automation, 166, 186
Average Revenue Per User (ARPU), 63
Awareness, 48

Babin, Leif, 122
Bandwidth management, 164–165
Baudelaire, Charles, 22
Bespoke account experience
  customized content, 103–108
  delivering customized demos, workshops/proposals, 115–119
  designing high-touch engagements, 108–112
  developing content and messaging, 97–103
  executing outreach campaigns, 112–115

Bespoke experience
account expectations, 42–52
high-value deals, generic messaging in, 40–42
hyperpersonalization, tangible ROI of, 36–40
key decision makers, building trust and rapport with, 34–36
modern business relationships, 32–33
1:1 ABM, personalization and customization in, 52–55
strategic messaging ≠ campaign slogans, 31–32
Bleustein-Blanchet, Marcel, 2
Brand voice, 102
Branding, 92, 99, 161
Branson, Sir Richard, 67
Brown, David, 38
Budgeting, 164–165
Building consensus/gaining stakeholder buy-in, 77–78
Burgess, Bev, 11, 40, 171
Business, deep personalization in, 21–22
Business-to-business (B2B), 2, 3, 11, 14, 31, 58, 101, 134, 145, 147–160, 185
Buy-in and sponsorship, 161–162

Campaign slogans, 31–32
Center of Excellence (CoE), 140
The Challenger Sale: Taking Control of the Customer Conversation, 8, 64
Change, reputation, 5
Changes, adapting, 168–170
Chief Information Officer (CIO), 36
Chief Marketing Officers (CMOs), 17, 24, 52, 126
Churn Rate, 63
Coca-Cola, 19
Collaboration, 23, 128–134
Communication, 7, 90, 94–96, 101, 103, 104, 106, 128–134
Competitive analysis, 71
Consideration, 48
Consistency and quality, 167–168
Content management systems (CMS), 135
Content optimization agents, 27
COVID pandemic, 42
Crazy Egg, 116
C-suite executives, 31, 43, 50, 91, 99
Customer, 8, 19, 21–24, 32, 33, 36, 38, 42–44, 69, 70, 71, 80, 81, 83, 85, 94, 96, 99, 109, 118, 122, 142, 153, 156, 158, 161, 172–173, 178, 179, 180, 181, 183, 186
Customer-centricity, 23
Customer lifetime value (CLV), 39
and ABM, 158–159
Customer relationship management (CRM), 15, 21, 38, 51, 69–71, 81, 118, 135–139, 143–145, 157, 163, 178
Customization, 20, 31–32, 52–55, 97, 102, 103, 113, 116, 134, 139, 148, 162
Customized marketing, 55

Data, 34–35, 50, 81, 138, 139, 141–145, 160, 162–165, 168, 180, 182, 183, 186, 189, 192
Data backbone approach, 144
Data management, 162–164
Deal Acceleration, 39, 40
Strategic ABM, 100
Decision, 48
Decision Maker, 87, 89
Decision-Making Unit (DMU), 87–89
Deep account intelligence/ understanding
account teams, gleaning insights from, 82–86
mapping stakeholders/building personas, 87–94
researching target accounts, 79–82
understanding individual pain points, motivations/ communication styles, 94–96

Demand Generation, 31
DemandScience, 135, 136, 174
Detailed account personas, 90–92
Digital interactions, 43
Direct-to-consumer (D2C), 20
Discipline, 20, 72, 116, 130, 144, 164
Distinguishing 1:1, 13–15
Dixon, Matthew, 8, 64
Duffy, Gayle, 26

Effective teamwork, 18–19
80/20 rule, 39
Empathy, 3, 28, 39, 44, 45, 71, 112
Ending the War Between Sales and Marketing, 121
Engagement monitoring agents, 27
Events, 161
Evidence, 77
Executive alignment, 68
Executive Sponsors, 68
Extreme Ownership, 122

Fake personalization, 18
Field Service Management, 32
Fowler, Jim, 144
Fox Plumbing & Heating, 38

Gen AI, 182–183
General Data Protection Regulation (GDPR), 119
Go-to-Market (GTM), 161, 172
Google search, 104
Gosling, Dorothea, 40
GPS, 93
Great ABM, 98

Heraclitus, 168
High-touch engagements, 108–112
High-touch interactions, 51–52
High-value deals, generic messaging in, 40–42
Hotjar, 116
HTML e-mail, 21, 50
Human connection, 2, 27, 92
Hyper-customization, 116
Hyperpersonalization, 36–40

Ideal Client Profile (ICP), 58
Ideal customer profile, 62
Ideal Strategic Account Profile (ISAP), 58–62, 143
  ABM framework, 59
  worksheet, 72
Identification, strategic accounts, 68–74
Implementation, 48, 165
Implementing 1:1 ABM operations
  aligning sales/marketing, 121–122
  collaboration, 128–134
  communication, 128–134
  shared goals, KPIs/revenue targets, 122–128
  technology, 134–145
  tools, 134–145
Industry analysis, 71–72
The Inflexion Group, 3, 40
Information gathering, 79
Intent data, 82

Joint account, 126–128
Jordan, Evan, 7

Key decision makers, 34–36
Key performance indicators (KPIs), 45, 122–124, 171–173
Kotler, Philip, 45–46, 121
Kreme, Krispy, 68
Krishnaswamy, Suj, 45–46, 121
KRISPIN Marketing, 149

Large Language Models (LLM), 182
Lead Gen funnel *vs.* ABM funnel, 23
Lead Generation, 161, 172
Leadership, 3, 21, 24, 25, 34, 40, 43, 48, 51, 58, 61, 68, 75, 77, 79–80, 86, 89, 98, 99, 110, 112, 114, 118, 122, 129, 132, 133, 140, 141, 142, 150, 154, 157, 158, 160–162, 172, 180, 183, 184
Learning from mistakes, 149–150
Leveraging internal data, 69–71
Lifetime value (LTV), 63
LinkedIn, 90
Long-term Strategic ABM, 5

Making connections, 44
Malhotra, Naresh, 71–72
Manual personalization, 28
Market research, 71–72
Marketing, 121–122, 125, 128
Marketing automation, 143, 144
Marketing Research: An Applied Orientation, 71–72
Martech landscape, 137
Maslow's Hierarchy of Strategic ABM Needs, 133
Master Service Agreement (MSA), 58
McGrotty, Kyle, 13, 37
Measurement, 24
  analytics, 143
Mentors, 25–26
Mergers and acquisitions (M&A), 86
Microsoft Teams, 28, 83
Misalignment, 57
Modern business relationships, 32–33
Motivations, 94–96

Net profit margin (NPM), 178
NTT Ltd, 13, 24, 26, 106, 155

Onboarding, 21, 45–46, 58, 63, 65, 74, 84, 85
1:1 engagement, prioritization frameworks for, 74–77
"One-size-fits-all" approach, 16, 21, 33, 98
The One to One Future: Building Relationships One Customer at a Time (1993, 5), 2
Onion Model, 62

Pain points, 94–96
Partners, 25–26
Patriot Jet, 19
Peppers, Don, 2
Personalization, 24, 33, 42–43, 52–55, 95, 102, 103, 113, 139–141, 144, 162, 183, 185
Post-COVID, 42
Precision empathy, 28–29
Preschern, Matt, 24
Proper account selection, 57–68
Public Relations Agency of Record (AOR), 67

Qualitative metrics, 173
Quantitative metrics, 173
Quarterly business reviews (QBRs), 153

Rackham, Neil, 45–46, 121
Relationship agents, 27
Relationships, 3, 5, 34, 92–94, 110, 131, 132, 133, 138, 147–149, 150, 153–155, 158, 165, 169, 172, 175, 176, 179, 181–185
Relevance, 2, 20, 27, 31–33, 38, 39, 45, 46, 51, 64, 66, 71, 76, 88, 99, 101, 103, 105, 115–117, 133, 149, 181, 185
Reputation, 3, 5, 131, 141, 167
Resource allocation, 164–165
Resource plan, 165
Revenue, 3–6, 131, 141, 143, 147, 148, 150, 154, 155, 158, 160–162, 164, 166, 171–181
Revenue targets, 122–123
Rhetorical triangle, 150–151
Rogers, Martha, 2
ROI, 14, 21, 31, 58, 63, 99, 101, 116, 135, 136, 147, 152, 157–160, 171, 178–179
  hyperpersonalization, 36–40
Ross, Bob, 169

Sales, 121–122, 125, 128
  marketing, 164
Sales ABM questionnaire, 47
The Sales Cycle Length, 112, 123
Sales intelligence, 144
Sales intelligence tools, 143
Sales teams, 77, 83, 124, 126, 131, 180
Salesforce Agentic AI Certification, 27
Scalability, 54, 166
Seattle's Seafair event, 19
Senior leadership, 21, 34, 51, 75, 89, 110, 122, 129, 132, 133, 150, 160–162

Senior vice president (SVP), 37
Service/Execution team, 83
Setbacks, 168–170
Shared KPIs, 123–124
Shared revenue forecasting model, 124
Social Penetration Theory (SPT), 62
Stakeholders, 16, 19, 21, 25, 31, 40, 41, 46, 48, 51, 66, 68, 77–78, 86, 87–94, 101, 107, 109, 110, 112, 115, 133, 140, 169, 179–181
"Start With Why" philosophy, 175
Strategic ABM, 156–158, 160–165, 167, 169, 171
  Agentic AI, 26–29, 181–187
  bespoke conversations, from broad campaigns to, 2–3
  business, deep personalization in, 21–22
  customized vs. personalized outreach, 182
  definition of, 8–10
  early experiments and my learnings in, 24–26
  emerging trends, 182
  evolution of, 10–13
  high-value accounts, 16–17
  major health insurance provider, 84
  Maslow's Hierarchy of Strategic, 133
  1:Few and 1:Many, Distinguishing 1:1 from, 13–15
  personalization and customization in, 52–55
  quote from sales, 130
  strategic account engagement, 22–24
  three R's of, 3–6
  timeline, 111
  white- glove experiences, 19–20
  white-glove treatment, 17–19
Strategic account engagement, 22–24
Strategic accounts
  building consensus/gaining stakeholder buy-in, 77–78
  identification, practical methods for, 68–74
  1:1 engagement, prioritization frameworks for, 74–77
  proper account selection, 57–68
Strategic messaging, 31–32
Strategic mindset, 148
Success metrics, 171–173
Survey Monkey/Microsoft Forms, 129

Tantry, Sathvik, 52
Target accounts, 7, 12, 16, 19, 21, 22, 25, 33, 41, 49, 52–54, 57–59, 62–64, 66, 69–71, 73, 79–82, 97, 106–109, 115, 117, 119, 121, 125, 126, 131, 132, 134–140, 142, 148, 150, 153, 156–158, 162, 163, 166–169, 171, 179, 182, 184, 186–189, 192, 193
Targeted engagement, 24
Technology, 134–145
Three-letter acronym (TLA), 181
Three R's, 3–6
Tools, 134–145
Top of Mind (ToM), 110
Total contract value (TCV), 160
Transparency, 44, 121, 124, 162
Trust, 18, 34–36, 46, 125, 129, 163, 167, 180, 183, 186, 187

Urchin Tracking Modules (UTMs), 157

Value creation, 46
The Value of Thought Leadership 2025 report, 150

White-glove experiences, 19–20, 155–160
White-glove treatment, 17–19
Williams, Sara, 128
Willink, Jocko, 122
Wilson, Stuart, 98

Zig Ziglar's quote, 57